ISSUES AND FRAGMENTS

ISSUES AND FRAGMENTS

Lucian Krukowski

RESOURCE *Publications* • Eugene, Oregon

ISSUES AND FRAGMENTS

Copyright © 2016 Lucian Krukowski. All rights reserved. Except for brief quotations in critical publications or reviews, no part of this book may be reproduced in any manner without prior written permission from the publisher. Write: Permissions, Wipf and Stock Publishers, 199 W. 8th Ave., Suite 3, Eugene, OR 97401.

Resource Publications
An Imprint of Wipf and Stock Publishers
199 W. 8th Ave., Suite 3
Eugene, OR 97401

www.wipfandstock.com

PAPERBACK ISBN: 978-1-4982-9628-1
HARDCOVER ISBN: 978-1-4982-9630-4
EBOOK ISBN: 978-1-4982-9629-8

Manufactured in the U.S.A.

CONTENTS

I—Will | 1
II—More on Will | 6
III—The Given | 22
IV—Giving | 28
V—Taking | 30
VI—Erlebs and Qualia | 31
VII—Wittgenstein on Silence | 35
VIII—Comparisons—Constraints | 49
IX—More on Silence | 51
X—Crooked and Straight | 56
XI—Walks for the Taking | 60
XII—The Good | 72
XIII—Passages | 80
XIV—Memories | 86
XV—Qualities of People I Hate | 98
XVI—A Different Passage | 103
XVII—Eternity | 108
XVIII—The Place for Everyone | 112
XIX—Life and Death | 114
XX—Confessions | 122
XXI—Beyond Poetry | 126
XXII—The New Purgatory (Preface) | 127
XXIII—Quod Est Demonstrandum | 132
XXIV—The New Purgatory (Issues) | 135
XXV—The New Purgatory (Fragments) | 137
XXVI—At One Remove | 143

CONTENTS

XXVII—How It Is There | 144
XXVIII—A Garden of Flowers | 146
XXIX—My Shark—My Love | 148
XXX—Singing For Spaghetti | 150
XXXI—Requiem | 153
XXXII—God | 155
XXXIII—Four Concepts Of God | 164
XXXIV—Interlude | 170
XXXV—Love And Death | 173
XXXVI—A Last Fragment | 180

I

WILL

As is the custom, I begin with God.

My first question is whether, in a system so patently monistic as the Heavenly Kingdom, there is any room for dualities—oppositions arising from inquiry into God's Will.

Upon preliminary reflection, the answer would be "no." Considering the extant account of Divine Characteristics: Omnipotence, Omniscience, Omni-benevolence—the distinction between God's Will and other of God's powers that would modify or oppose it may not be one to make. To will and not to act, i.e., is not God's way—to will, for an omnipotent God, just is to act. As God's temporality is not that of humans—God being eternal—there is no "antecedent," "subsequent," or "consequent" relationship between the two—willing and acting. Movement and stasis are the same. This consideration arises from the nature of God's other powers. Omniscience precludes a need for probabilistic prediction—or the problem of incomplete recall; and omni-benevolence counters moral uncertainty—the search for gradations between virtue and vice.

My question continues into other aspects of Divinity: God and Heaven may both be eternal, but somewhere along the line—as the story goes—the arch-angel Lucifer went bad, and Hell needed God for its creating—a first-place that is outside of Heaven—an "elsewhere" that houses the first exemplar of sin and evil and so embodies the, here-to-for unneeded, principle of "punishment." When did punishment begin? The Devil—qua "evil"—was not manifest throughout all eternity. So the concept of "when" enters here, and implies the measuring of "time." Temporality—even of the Heavenly kind, can then be approached as a "late" sub-species of eternity—just before the world began.

Surely, there was a pre-temporal steady state before the occurrence of the two revolts in Heaven—the diabolical—when Satan rebelled, and the human—when Eve bit the apple, and Adam dutifully followed. As regards the heavenly "when," we might conjecture that the Devil was already consigned to Hell before his temptation of Eve—and then, in accordance with his now bifurcated and newly flexible will, proceeded to act by slithering silently through an unguarded worm-hole back into Paradise. There must (by then) indubitably have been a "then"—so the temptation of God's created couple marks the advent of human time in Paradise. It also marks the first exercise of human will—and its contingent consequences: Eve first wanted the apple—then she took it. After that, she offered a bite to Adam—whereupon he took one too. And then, as a first instance of later masculine misogyny, he blamed the consequences—on her. This separation of will and act marks the first occurrence of physical time—when our forbears were expelled from the ideality of Paradise, and trudged into our world.

But before we continue on with "us," we will stay in heaven a bit longer—other aspects of the story need addressing: One such is the occurrence of the Diabolical in Paradise. Within the previous scope of omni-benevolence, a dissident note is interjected. But why does it come—and from where? This intrusion—whether seen as an internally ignored privation, or as independently emanating from outside Heaven—exemplifies the earliest tension—a needed choice—between willing and acting. Evil requires an action—Good does not. Does Evil then, somehow—at some point—emanate from within the Good that exemplifies the Kingdom of Heaven? Or was it (timelessly) there "all along"—thereby identifying dualism as the central characteristic of both eternal essence and physical existence—as in the Zoroastrian duality of good and evil—Ormadzd contra Ahriman? The Devil must have thought (willed) rebellion before he acted; and God certainly didn't create Hell before it was needed. The "before," here, implies a temporal intrusion into the eternal realm.

Within a monistic view of the Divine characteristic of omni-benevolence, willing and doing are always good. But this suggests another tension—between omni-benevolence and omniscience. The question can be asked in two ways: "Does" God—qua eternal—or "did" God—qua temporal—know of the Devil's will to rebel? If not—given the scope of omniscience—why not? But if God knows or knew—why, given the scope of omnipotence, was it allowed to happen?

We ask further what the Devil hoped to accomplish, what he knew and why he failed (the first instance of failure?) thereby emphasizing the emergence of a further separation between will and act, motive and consequence. So we now have two new entities: A first (moment of) time and a first failure.

These difficulties need not—although they may—indicate a lessening in Divine Power. More interestingly, they could reveal (to us) that eternity contains a developmental principle, a character of change—however this is distinguished from our worldly notions of physical time and causality—a changing that permits such notions as expansion, enrichment, rejection, destruction, sublation, to be included in the divine reality. The Hegelian undertones here are deliberate. I will take them up shortly.

But if a paradise that is developmental doesn't fit one's concept of eternity—the above-noted difficulties remain. Then the traditional scenario returns: God in Heaven wins the war with evil—and banishes the Devil to (a God-created) Hell. Mortals—kicked out of Paradise—are given the treacherous capacity of free will—the choice between good and evil—thereby assuring the subsequent distribution of their souls between Heaven and Hell. This raises more questions: Why is God's victory over Satan only partial? Why is Satan still around? Was there free will in Heaven before the fall? Or was Eve the first free-willer? Given theological satisfaction of these pre-creation difficulties, we still ask: Why, given God's omni-benevolence, does this persistence of evil continue to scripturally present mortals with the ongoing threat of a dreadful Hell, surfeit with agony and hopelessness for all eternity? And why does it encourage (through heavenly acquiescence) the strife between the hapless, the weak, the smug, and the vicious—so de-facto underwriting the worldly contest between those who profit from sin and those who are its victims?

Also: It would seem that God, given the triumvirate of absolute power, knowledge, and compassion, could have willed the Devil and his Hell to not be—or to not ever having been.

ISSUES AND FRAGMENTS

That God did not do so, identifies the (concept of the) Devil as a source for the dichotomy between will and act. This can be taken as a symbol—a harbinger in fact—of a new stage in the developmental concept of eternity. It is the Devil's entrance into our drama that allows time and possibility to effect their separation from the mode (eternal actuality) of an earlier Heaven. But this also gives the Devil, whatever his singular will demands, a more salubrious task. To further the story, I suggest this: By instantiating evil, the Devil generates action-in-time, and so can be considered an efficient cause in divine teleology—a cause that puts Heaven in motion. Perhaps this is what God has in mind.

Will, for the human mind, is a salient characteristic of the natural world. In theory, it deviates from the Divine Will in certain important respects: We may believe we are omnipotent and so we will an action believing that it can be done. But as we are not omniscient, we cannot know this with certainty. So we hesitate—which takes time—and we turn for support to our restricted human form of omni-benevolence—enlightened self-interest. We then ask: Is this projected action in our best interests—and (on the whole) in (most) everyone else's? This (temporal) interplay of dependencies and frictions between will and action is a—perhaps the—defining characteristic of human rationality.

But "rationality," of course, is not a given. It is only a description of how we sometimes justify ourselves—rationalize the actions that are consequent on our willing—by finding good reasons for them. There are alternatives: Others prefer to act from bad reasons—stemming from a love for "irrationality." Still others just find reasons that are based on "reality"—which can be most anything that is useful.

In the above, I have given a developmental slant to Divinity's contribution to the question of "will." This, for secular thinkers, may certainly seem fanciful. But I offer this additional consideration: The immense struggle that has marked the transition from religious mythology to philosophic rationality to contemporary materialism—also documents the historical voyage of our notion of will—its nature, origins, limits, and its connection to the actions it provokes. It is central to the concerns of moral theory. From another standpoint, this struggle to understand (control—encourage) volition reveals the relationship of will to its antithesis—death. From still another vantage—a strongly materialistic one—the notion of a "free" will brings into question, through neurological investigations, as to whether there is a will at all—or whether the term "will" is now obsolete (except as a metaphor for otherwise causally explicable actions). In this last context, "will" is poetically useful as a basis for the description of human choice.

    Will, considered as a "creative," and so autonomous faculty, is a "mind" term. Considered as physiologically traceable behavior, it is a "brain" term.

II

MORE ON WILL

AT THIS POINT, I comment on some philosophical theories that show particular sensitivity to historical changes in the construal of will.

Kant

I begin with Immanuel Kant. In his "Metaphysics of Morals" (1785), Kant starts his discussion on will with this statement: "Nothing in the world—indeed nothing even beyond the world—can possibly be conceived which could be called good without qualification except a Good Will." Here, I want to refer this—to us familiar—statement to some qualifications that contribute to the contrasts I want to make.

Kant's ideal will is good—not happy—and its pursuit is a measure of personal character, not of worldly achievement. It is perfectly possible to have a miserable life while pursuing the goal of a good will. It is also possible to have a materially fulfilled life without regard for the goodness of one's willing. The propelling factor in the measure of a good will is a good character that, for Kant, is an introspective rather than a social measurement—although its achievement is—in principle—universally desirable, but only sometimes discernable.

Here, the theory's passivity as regards external engagement shows itself. Kant is skeptical that individual action can be sufficiently decontaminated of personal ambition to achieve the exercising of a completely good will. He distinguishes sharply between the empirical world and its determining principle of causality, and the intelligible world whose principle is freedom. Although humans consist of both worlds, the moral life is based on the latter—through the categorical (universalizing) test of motives for action. Appetite contends with reason as a motive for moral action—the "good will" is an outcome of the worked-for priority of reason.

Accordingly, Kant recommends the contemplative life—the rational concern with the moral clarification of will—as the proper life. This is also the habitat of the recluse saint and is an indication of Kant's resistance (a theological residue?) to the moral equating of "good" and "happy"—as a goal for living. Only the artist—qua "genius"—to which Kant gives the status of a "force of nature," escapes the ambivalence (and incipient privations) of will.

I now turn to another of Kant's writings. In beginning his essay "What is Enlightenment?" (1784) Kant states that the motto of Enlightenment is "Sapere Audi ("Dare to be wise" [Horace]). But a few pages later he comments: "Only one prince (Frederick) in the world says; Argue as much as you will, and about what you will, but obey." Kant's quotation emphasizes his own reticence about social engagement. In the following pages, Kant repeatedly identifies Frederick's "you" as the "scholar." This distinction between "willing" (arguing for) and "doing" (acting) is central to Kantian ethics. We have the (rational) obligation to the good will as if it were a divine dictate—but we do not have the (material) capacity to accomplish what we rationally will. Even in the most extended arena of the good-will—Kant's "Kingdom of Ends"—the particular intrudes. We may, or may not, admit our moral frailty—this is an ethical dilemma. But, living-in-the-world, we stake our individual survival on expedience—the consequence-laden, hypothetical judgment—"if-then"—of particular willing. This is a problem for the moral life: From the vantage of our needs and desires, if we were to view the demands of the categorically good will, it would follow that we would not want the implementation (by us—for us) of a universally (collectively) good will—for then we would be (self) obligated to act according to its (purely) rational dictates—often against our own particular interests. The actual implementation of a categorical imperative, so read, entails a voluntary loss of freedom. But, then, how can eschewing freedom be voluntary?

We can distance this question, by taking it off our backs and putting it onto the shoulders of all inhabitants of the developing "Kingdom-of-Ends." We all will do what we can—and hope that our "doing" gets better in the long run.

We can then hold the "good will" as an ideal for some indefinite future—as an infinite task. But, as regards our own behavior, we can find solace in Saint Augustine, who reputedly said—"soon, but not yet, Lord—not yet."

To "argue yet obey," refers to the limits of Kant's own society and also to a benign Jehovah—who is in it for the long run. The Divine Will, however, is inscrutable as to how it works in human affairs. Frederick's mandates are maxims of the (benign) Imperial will—which must be obeyed—they are the best possible so far. But such obeying is more difficult in a despotic society—or in the absence of an adequate location of will's basic source of rationality.

This last is philosophically germane. For the individual, the questions are: How can we know that our will is good? How can we make it better? The first is a philosophical question; the second is a socio-ethical question. For the first, we can rely either on a self-given, a-priori judgment, or through appeal to a divine power. For the second, there are two standard suggestions: One—Education in rationality; Two—Indoctrination of true belief. These both have serious problems: Despite our many efforts, moral education has had but limited success. Indoctrination in "proper" behavior is more efficient, but smacks of totalitarianism. Here is a recently finessed third suggestion: Persuasiveness through marketing—which is now our most successful effort in indoctrination: Give them what they (think they) want, and they will do what (you think) is right. For all such contexts, however, Kant's moral law remains dualistic—in that the goodness of will vacillates between the rational authority of maxims, and the contingent willing of actions. There may, however, be another way to do the numbers.

Kant's subdivisions throughout his critiques are mainly of two and multiples of two. But in his moral theory we can read an intrusive and yet, premonitory, suggestion of three: There is the moral law itself—universal for every context. Then there are the derivative maxims—determinants or rules for the specific issues (human actions) that raise moral questions. Further (or below) there are the acts themselves—whose causalities (consequences of willing) cannot be totally adjudicated through the maxims that occupy the unhappy (historical-legalistic) middle ground between universal law and specific act.

This triadic interpretation, if put in motion, is a harbinger of Hegel—to whom I now turn.

MORE ON WILL

Hegel

Kant avoids time (development) in his formulation of the purely good will. He admits time into the exercise of the contingent will—but offers only the exercise of rationality as the path to (the certainty of) goodness. Such certainty, however, has a metaphysical status—it is beyond achievement, and so, beyond time. The effort to achieve the Good stays with the individual consciousness as its rational task—where it must compete with desire as a stimulus for action.

Hegel, in contrast, does not much consider individual willing as an essential factor in historical developmental. The "Evolution of Spirit" (Phenomenology, 1807) is, in a sense, impersonal. People variously do what they want and can—but the development through ascending stages of culture happens inevitably—regardless of particular historical and personal motives, actions, or events. Although Hegel's influence on later totalitarianisms has been much noted—here I consider his dialectic thesis from another point of view—that of a (last) great teleological strategy for the synthesis of human culture with the divine plan: Hegel's "Geist" evolves into a reunification with it's source—God. Along the way, it divests itself of physicality, individuality, and particular willing—it becomes pure spirit. This process, as evidenced in human history, is called "progress" and is present in all cultural forms. In art, the evolution culminates in the purely verbal arts—prose, poetry. The concrete materials of the plastic arts, and their reliance on handicraft and strategies of representation, are progressively discarded as art ascends from the ancient, heavily material works—the temples and "grotesques"—of far-Eastern Symbolic art, through a (momentarily) perfect synthesis of form and material in ancient Greece, to the freedom of "pure thought" in modern poetry.

But Hegel was too acute to conflate aesthetic value with dialectic necessity. Some old art may be more compelling—indeed better—than the newer forms. For him, Classical Greek sculpture is the most perfect art—qua art—of all the historical offerings in that it shows a balanced conciliation (gesture of content and architectonic stability) between spirit and matter. But the importance of old art for the needs of new cultures lessens as the dialectic continues. New art may symbolically be more purified than old art, but of a lesser significance for the larger concepts of the new culture. For Hegel, art—as with other cultural forms—is developmentally finite. Beyond the limits of art, progress continues through the still-descriptive images of religious thought—until it evolves into the rarified and purified realm of philosophy: Thought (adequately—finally) thinking itself.

Hegel finds morality in the dialectic—an impersonal morality—which is not so much an imposition of the moral law in the specific circumstance as it is an awareness of transition between both circumstances and beliefs—which leads, in the long run—to a purification of motive (will) and an increase in the moral caliber of the consequent act. To go back: Kant views betterment—the increase of "goodness" in the general will—to be consequent on a questionably achievable increase in secular rationality. Hegel, instead, believes the achievement is a given—found in the teleological nature of the march of history—a sublation of lesser into higher cultures that tends towards a unity—a one (finally sacral) world—where there is no longer need, or place, for conflict between individual willing.

But what is the source of the "given" in this process? After Kant, it became difficult to talk sensibly of an immanent, intrusive God. So Hegel transformed The Divine Will, formerly instigator and consequence of moral development, into a universal historical process which, nevertheless, remains value-laden: The world progresses through self-purification—(How else to speak of "worse" and "better?")—although its events are formative-of—not formed-by—the exercise of individual will. But in this scenario of a progressing world, the issue of its source—the nature and reasons for development—the "originator" of this process—remains obscure. In this sense, Hegel is more like Aristotle than Aquinas.

I don't think that Hegel had much interest in a Divinity—except as manifested in historical imagery. He took great pains to document the historical changes in both material and concept. The "evolution of spirit" could indeed be presented first as an event—thus requiring a beginning, an end—and some form of divine willing. But, taking a leaf from Aristotle: The "four causes" are ways to analyze specific processes—selected out of a continuum. "First" and "Final," in this sense, are methodological (linguistic) limits imposed on the area of consideration. They are not, as I see it, reifications of evolutionary process as being the internal workings of a finite unity—with God as the infinite reason. We remember that neither Heraclitus nor Democritus required such encapsulation for their descriptions of flux. Infinity—without cause or consequence—did not frighten them as it did the later Christian apologists. And Hegel was particularly fond of the ancient Greeks.

Hegel's theory of historical development has of course been interpreted in purely, even adamantly, secular terms—with consequences we are still living through. But such interpretations—most notably, Marxism—also raise the skeptical question of the value of a developmental totalitarianism. Put simply: One that knows where we are (should be) headed. What, then, is the difference between a good will that embraces the (theoretical) course of history, and a free will that would deny its inevitability? Or, as in Kant—a will that is free to argue for the universal "good," yet required to acknowledge its limitations in the actual case.

Schopenhauer

Schopenhauer, much as he admired Kant, had no truck with a "good will." Willing is bad—it is the basis for aggression, cupidity, sexual license, and all the other depravities that humans have, want, and are likely to exhibit in the course of living. Schopenhauer is an unrepentant dualist—of which pairing, will, occupies one—the distaff—side. For him, "will" cannot be educated, pacified, or reformed. It is a given—the destructive part of the human psyche. Within its sway, there is no teleology, no development in history—only an incessant appetitive striving which is never assuaged and which has no goal beyond its satisfaction. History, correspondingly, has neither reason nor purpose. Even the empirical sciences, while they increase knowledge, do not generate progress through their findings—they only provide increased alternatives for the satisfaction of will's appetites. This tension between knowledge and behavior remains a fundamental question for current attempts to correlate scientific progress with an increase in moral understanding.

Schopenhauer's concern with the duplicity of will is so extreme that it can be construed as a disbelief that what one consciously wills is the actual motive for the consequent action: One never knows what one "really" wants, or why one does what one does. This gives rise to the notion of a "hidden will" (not accessible to reason) that is the source of the unconscious desires—the true bases for our actions. This notion is an "Intuitionist" theory in that a number of ways of knowing are required to encompass Schopenhauer's ontological triad of "will," "forms," and "matter." He makes little attempt to present an epistemic sub-structure from which all these ways can be derived. Indeed, he often hints at a solipsism: "The world is my thought"—perhaps as a way of defending against the power of a pervasive metaphysical will as it is manifest in human behavior. Only a sur-reality of eternal and timeless "Forms" or "Ideas" (even when provided solely by the mind) that, we believe, underlays the transient and destructive realities of will—can protect us from the blandishments of "progress in history" and its concomitant evils. Schopenhauer really disliked Hegel.

Schopenhauer was well versed in the physical sciences, and had no quarrel with scientific method and its findings. "Will," however, he regarded as both an underlying and yet an immediate, visceral manifestation in both the social and natural processes of the external world. But will is outside culture—it cannot be tamed—it is the antithesis to rationality. For the individual self, the will is recognized (for what it is) through introspection—a questioning of the motives that underlie one's own actions. It is only through denying the will, and rejecting its powers over the self, that one can come to (a semblance of) peace and tranquility—the realm of "Ideas."

This projection of a divided psyche is, of course, a precursor of the Freudian theory of the sub-conscious and it's many mischiefs. The "hiddenness" of our reasons for willing can be turned into the extreme position—within which we are not aware of the "real-reasons" for our acting—or even for (rationally) thinking about the consequences of our actions. From a psychiatric viewpoint, this identifies a psychosis—for it involves an abnegation of responsibility for one's very being—and results in an ensuing sense of powerlessness—and the desire for death. It also carries a realization of cosmic indifference to human acts. This realization is a contributing factor in Schopenhauer's atheism.

To my mind, the consequences of will in Schopenhauer's philosophy are dangerous to entertain—for they locate every finding, every assertion, as ultimately resting on a sub-rational, putatively malevolent, source—hidden from both the individual and the greater society. But the emphasis on an unbridled will can also produce a militant nihilism that finds a different expression in Nietzsche.

Schopenhauer does not seek the terrain of Nietzsche's nihilism. His pessimism is more personal than metaphysical. He is more interested in the duplicity of the individual will than in the irrationality of the world. So instead, he challenges Kant's Enlightenment optimism by asking, in effect: Why is it that the moral law is so irrelevant to action? Why is will so impervious to morality?

To escape the impasse, (for he much admired Kant) Schopenhauer posits another realm that is outside the purview of will—the realm of "ideas"—particularly as it is manifested in the appreciation of art—especially in music.

This other side of Schopenhauer's philosophy—the idea—constitutes a realm which is untainted by will, and represents existence through a presentation of forms, or essences, that are outside the processes of conflict and change. These processes are negatively identified with the workings of the Hegelian theme of "progress"—that (amoral) willing—when it is presented as the source of historically determined living. Will, for Schopenhauer, is indifferent to the historical residue of the victims of its workings—it has no ethical dimension. This points to the deep differences between Schopenhauer's philosophy and that of his contemporary—Hegel.

Schopenhauer's rejection of teleology in history—and his vilification of the principle of will—shows the need for another construct to save his philosophy from a pervasive pessimism. This he does through the thesis of an alternate reality—a will-less, world of forms—which, while they represent the dynamics of life, do not actually embody them—rather, they are life's rational source.

One source of Schopenhauer's theory of ideas is, of course, the Platonic theory of the "Eternal Forms." But while Plato locates his forms in a transcendent realm—the "place beyond the heavens"—Schopenhauer approaches his ideas in a manner closer to that of a Buddhist monk—through a contemplation of, rather than an engagement with, life. Adopting this attitude of passivity and denial shows an evident skepticism as regards progress, and so, rejects the value of worldly ambition. Yet, in compensation for this withdrawal, there remains the gratification of living when taken as an undivided nature abstracted from physical volition. While one cannot use will to not will—in this move of withdrawal, will need not be abolished—rather, its power can be negated through purification—a redirection from things to their essence—from striving to contemplation. This move is an echo of Kant's "disinterested (aesthetic) perception" in his "Critique of Judgment."

ISSUES AND FRAGMENTS

In a more extreme reading, however, the predatory nihilistic will must be otherwise negated—through a power that casts the Devil down. (Saint Michael putting the sword to the Serpent). But the abnegation of will, and the corresponding move from will to idea cannot be appealed to through the will's own "willingness." The doctrine of forms requires an additional realm—independent of will—that would provide the necessary locus and rationale for the movement from will to its negation. This is the realm of the Idea. Schopenhauer seems content with this separation of realms, for he does not give us any philosophical strategy through which his contesting realms can be reconciled. Perhaps he did not think that unity is a virtue—or perhaps he thought, as is more probable, that philosophy ends at this point.

Schopenhauer loved music—not only because he enjoyed it—he was too thoughtful—but because, for him, music more purely shows the sheer form of willing than does any other art. In its ascending and descending, fortes and pianos, harmonies and dissonances, conclusions and recapitulations, music provides the semblance of will-in-time without its actual instantiations in life. Schopenhauer evidently was precocious in understanding the power of abstraction in art. Listening to music permits us (if only for a time) to escape the workings of (our own) will through the appreciation of the (purified) willing that is analogously presented in music. This is a distinction between exemplification and expression—between showing and having, between fiction and actuality. The form of fiction has this advantage over the form of life: Art—whatever the medium—exists in the time peculiar to its representation: painting in the present-eternal of depiction; music in the compressed and articulated time of the vagaries of living; poetry in the ruminative time of the reader's thought. In Schopenhauer's philosophy, music has the privileged position of being sensual, evocative, and yet benign. We learn something about our living from the abstraction of life that is encapsulated in music. Musical sequence is a condensation of a sequence of living, which—as in all art—is partial, and often inadequate. But "adequacy"—in both life and art—is a value judgment. The capacity for "appreciation" becomes a factor here: The types and varieties of musical representation we most respond to provide a measure of how we view our own lives.

This move by the psyche, belabored by will, to the idealities shown in music, is a victory over nihilism—one that, in Schopenhauer's time, art could still provide. But music, in its workings for a represented actuality, is not a substitute for the living will. It is only an escape, or possibly a tutorial—so the deeper pessimism remains. There is, in this, a negative judgment about the power of rationality to cope with reality. There is also the internalizing aesthetic denial that life is preferable to art—a reason (for others) for laughter.

Nietzsche

Nietzsche prized Schopenhauer for his pessimism and his atheism. Schopenhauer had rid philosophy of God and of teleology—no trans-worldly divinity is needed, and no historical purpose is to be found. But then—the question still arises—what is left for meaning and purpose? Nietzsche centers the answer on his recognition of a fundamental lack—a disconnect between the continuity of past and future which serves to render the present vacuous. This dilemma is central to Nietzsche's thesis of the "Death-of-God." The past can be remembered but not relived—and without forgiveness, we cannot become other than what we then already were—wrapped in our weakness. Without God, the future is equally punishing—for it is neither conversant with the past nor can it be trusted to create a reality more rational than the conflicted one of our present.

Paradoxically, Nietzsche turns this negativity into joy. He transforms the duplicitous psychological will into one of pre-history and legend. He changes the subconscious origins of Schopenhauer's will into mythical ones of an ancient past: (Also Sprach Zarathustra, 1883-85). Nietzsche's will permeates and gathers together all of reality—past and future. He calls it the "will to power," and locates it in the workings of the natural world as well as in human society.

But to extend this claim into history, Nietzsche's "will" must reclaim the past and capture the future by re-locating both—finding their realities—in the present. Here, he offers the difficult thesis of "the Eternal Return"—a transformation (better—appropriation) of time's linear path into a circular form. This gambit requires a "two-fold" will—one that succeeds in returning to the past and, through a fearless leap, brings it forward to join with-and-for the present. Then, in a still more perilous move, Nietzsche's "will" must reach ahead and coerce the future into an incipient commonality with the past-as-present. This is the "will to power" that underlies Zarathustra's accomplishment—to redeem everything in the past by re-creating "all that it was" into a "thus I willed it." It is also an admonition to the future that it is not unknowable—for it is nothing beyond its formulation in our present— "it will (then) be as I (now) will it." Such a conceit requires believing that willed power abrogates the linearity of time. It is a gesture toward replacing nihilism with myth by transforming time's line into a circle—so giving us control over our past and future. One must live as if the past and future become realized—fully knowable—fully changeable—in the present. Indeed, to stretch Nietzsche's point: The future becomes the past in that both are reconstituted by will's power into a now compliant present. Will thus assumes hegemony over time. Past regrets and future fears are vanquished by immolation in the present—a Liebestod—a joining—of love and death. Then, for Nietzsche—the rest is silence.

But there is evidence that Dionysus—in the battle with Apollo—has also won a few: Nietzsche's will-to-power is primed to supersede Kant's good will and Schopenhauer's malevolent will—and, if we follow its imperatives into the future—the free-will as well. But that is an irrelevant blaming of the past for the misdeeds of the future—while our life is completely in the present. In the time that Nietzsche gives him, Zarathustra greets the promise of this accomplishment with laughter—a God-free, Dionysian laughter that is aimed at shaming the faceless egalitarianism of Apollinian, Neo-Christian, eschatological thought.

Nietzsche admired Wagner—in particular the four-opera opus: "Der Ring Des Niebelungen," (1853-74)—which seemed to him to be a powerful artistic formulation of the coherence between—and a joining of—the factors of the "Eternal Return." But Wagner had his own ideas, and in "Parsifal" (and in his own life) returned to the linear eschatology of Christian myth: Redemption is sought-for through the search for the "holy grail."

For Nietzsche, this was a betrayal—and so he wrote "Contra Wagner" (1888-89)—an essay that condemns Wagner's move—and if nothing else, shows the joined power of art and philosophy at that time.

Post-Will

From the Medieval period through early modern time, will was understood as a "mental faculty—in keeping with, but independent of, the other human faculties—such as faith, reason and appetite. This equivocal relationship formed the basis for the theory of "faculty psychology"—an understanding

MORE ON WILL

of the human psyche through the interplay of its constituent parts. The theory developed many variants, but a major historical source can be traced back to Aristotle who, in "De Anima," spoke of various competing functions of the soul—and the possibilities (consequences) of their interaction.

The theory gained fuller force in the writings of Thomas Aquinas (Summa Theologica)—who identified the three major faculties as "intellect, will, and emotions." Importantly for Catholic doctrine, this sequestration of functions introduces the notion of a "transfer of training," where the proper exercises—logic, prayer, abstinence, and obedience—would strengthen and integrate the faculties of the mind in ways that are compatible with scripture. Within this framework, the theory is not merely descriptive but prescriptive—in that mental faculties had to be separately trained to reject all of: false belief, improper actions, sinful desires—before (so to speak) they could be freed to come together to mal-form a life. This imposition was deemed necessary for both social and doctrinal control—and for the promise of salvation. The harshness of death's inevitability in overcoming will, was then countered by the doctrine that a virtuous life leads to heaven—where souls are all equal in their bliss—and where there is no need for will.

The explanation of human function through division into faculties became a secular psychology in the eighteenth century. The Kantian division of science, morality, and art into separate critiques—each subject to further division through the fourfold categorical distinction of "quantity, quality, relationship, modality"—is for me, the high point of that form of explanation. Kant however, was not interested in a compartmentalization of human behavior—but in developing a schema through which one can understand the empirical world as well as its ethical component. Nevertheless, the explanatory power of "categories," and the judgments they generate, developed their own formal fascination—independent of specific applications.

The behavioral link between mental faculties, pre-dispositions, and resultant actions, as a form of psychological explanation, was largely abandoned in the twentieth century. But the impact of this theory continues in the organization of studies in universities through the division of curricula through "Faculties"—each with its own set of courses, and each in competition for the prize of "relevance" (the gold ring of the academic carousel). This model (while dismaying some) continues into the present day.

Its justification is through a categorizing of extant knowledge—historical, technical, and topical—rather than by appeal to the older theoretical distinctions between rationality, will, and emotion. I suspect, however, that these old distinctions lurk behind some of the new ones—if only as a fall back for our continuing justification.

The decline of faculty psychology (and the demise of its components as explanations of behavior) is a consequence of two theoretical changes. The first is the Freudian separation between drives and consciousness: The sub-conscious level of Id is largely inaccessible to the conscious level of Ego—thus making it resistant to understanding the origins of its contents, and thereby diminishing self-awareness and the encouragement to act in certain (rational) ways. The Super-Ego—that distillation of social and doctrinal prohibitions—in contrast, is all too evident to the Ego, where it is made manifest as admonition (from outside-made-inside) for bad behavior and unfulfilled obligations. In this drama, Id and Super-Ego are not subject to the willing of the Ego—the first is hidden underneath, the second is too aggressively outside. This constriction confirms the sense of powerlessness within the self. The articulation of this beleaguered self is no longer to be found in a "faculty" of Will—one that is a structural component (a defender) of the self. Rather, it is distributed across a pair of seemingly impersonal influences: Guilt on the bottom (Id) and duty (Super-Ego) above. Losing the assurance of (the efficacy of) "willing," leaves a more vulnerable self—more open to happenstance than to the firm and deliberate exercise of an autonomous "Will."

Yet, these power plays of Id, Ego, and Super-ego can also be seen as remnants of faculty psychology—the difference being that these Freudian faculties, so separated, are not under the control of the conscious will. Biblical analogues are the serpent and the expulsion from the Garden—the panoply of seduction and punishment. Continuing on in this fictional mode: The expulsion from paradise is but a moment—a fragment of physical time—but it is more real than the eternal time of paradise because of the opacity of its motive: What is God up to? Was disobedience—eating the forbidden fruit—the first act of human will? Was there a prior example (sample) in the heavens of the pleasure offered by the apple? Or was pleasure, as such, created as the content of temptation and desire—(biting the apple)—and so instantiated the first human emotion?

MORE ON WILL

The Talking-Cure (prayer, exhortation, analysis) has long been the weapon of enlightened choice against deviant willing. But the motives in most cases of deviance are opaque: They may be anti-cultural (often for political reasons) or they may be personally neurotic and so generate anti-social behavior. The public response to these "aberrations" typically vacillates between treatment and incarceration. The current psychiatric emphasis on diagnosis and drug therapy—rather than psychoanalysis—is a case in point: Analysis is too expensive and too lengthy a way to bring patients into betterment—even though medical research continues to have success in finding correlations between abnormal physiology and psychological pathologies. Analogously, acts of will and their mental origins can be defined through ethical or religious criteria—justifications of deviant acts may find the medical diagnosis inadequate for religious purposes. In all fairness, medical research has not shown—except in retrospect—how behavior is located in mental (brain) origins—nor can it predict the occurrence of individual volitions that determine future behavior. Some of these difficulties undoubtedly occur because of legal—individual privacy—concerns. Others may be charged to asking the wrong questions—a metaphysical fault. But the science is young—and it would be premature to reject it (although tempting) as a more sophisticated version of faculty psychology. Maybe, in the future, we will all be known—beforehand.

The most recent solution to the problem of mental categories is to abandon the concept of Faculty. There are no faculties—only behaviors—not traceable to, nor definable by, recourse to physical or meta-physical categories of mental function. This has its downside: It bodes poorly for family values, sexual prohibitions, altruism—and other long-held social virtues—none of which are (presently) locatable in the brain. The proper interpretation of a "faculty occurrence" was once regarded as a way of judging sanity, piety, honesty. Losing this assurance required other, more social, criteria—success, wealth, power, renown, and good publicity.

For me, there is some sadness in this transition.

So what is left, then—except in a poetic way—to say about the will? It once was a separate faculty with intersecting parts: A good will that is necessary for heroism, great thoughts, altruism; a strong will that is wanted for winning battles, political quarrels, and seductions; a malevolent will that foments chaos, evil, and oppression; a weak will that results in anomy and failure.

But these days, the term has receded from faculty status to every-day linguistic usage. Will is now a name for behavior that leads to any (or all) of the above. Perhaps it would be sufficient to omit all references to the will, and just talk about actions and re-actions. But the term persists. It is too resonant and melodramatic, too available for ordinary explanation to discard completely. So I look at its continuations in linguistic usage.

Consider the terms 'willing' and 'willful.' They both maintain the aura of earlier anxieties about the exercise of 'Will.' A willing worker (although uneasily) can be correlated with a willing victim—both are affirmative in their willing. The first condition is desirable (although workers are often victimized); the second is circumstantial (whether the victimization—so called—is malevolent or pleasurable). 'Unwilling'—as applied to worker, lover, or slave—can be understood through the latitude that is left to the will in each case, to change the unwanted circumstances. Following the Freudian triad, it might be that "willing to do," does not mean (or only partially overlaps) what one "wants to do." Subconscious fears and desires confront the demands of the public world. Beware! This power is not all external. We may not know what we (really) want to do in particular situations—but we know what we are willing to do, when we have "consciously" made that choice. The reasons one has (gives to one's-self) for any doing, may range from making the best of a bad situation (as in staying alive while submitting to rape) or decorating the front lawn with Christmas lights (because that's the custom of the neighborhood).

In such contexts, the hidden motives that influence action pose a problem for philosophical thought. Kant, with his own elaborate Critical Triad—each offering a particular form of knowledge (empirical truth, moral obligation, aesthetic insight)—would surely think that the idea of internal motives hidden to rational choice—is childish or duplicitous. Hegel would probably think that, in the long run, it doesn't matter—but would have welcomed such simple-believers to his lectures. (They came in droves). Schopenhauer would have understood the impasse between feuding categories—not least because he was a contributing influence—but also because he had the means to sit in a solitary place and listen to music. (Few came to his scheduled lectures). Nietzsche, I'm sure, would have been furious at this dilution of the power he wanted for his hero (and himself). Zarathustra came down from the mountain to teach an aggressive joy—immediate, uncompromised by memory or anxiety, undaunted by fears of the

MORE ON WILL

future, given support by the exploits of mythic heroes—a joy to be had in welcoming the conscious present—and attested to by feasting and laughter. Weakness he would not tolerate. Death, when it comes, becomes an immolation—effected by that last autonomous act of Will.

The term 'willful'—when stripped of its philosophical import—is ambiguous in popular usage: A willful child and a willful politician evidence (potential) disobedience as regards some or other social norms—but the jury is out until the behavior becomes manifest. Afterwards, the attribution 'willful' is taken as a character description that explains both past and future actions. The term—because it suggests an extreme—carries forebodings of danger, but also suggestions of promise—it depends on the present elections, or the child's end-term grades. Strangely, the contrary term— 'will-less'—is more difficult to apply. It can perhaps refer to someone in a catatonic state, or a saint brooding in the desert, or an inordinately placid person—a "couch potato"—but it is not a term in active use. I note that 'will-less' and 'willful' are not contradictories—they are contraries; "less" and "full" indicate degree of difference, not logical negation. The scarcity of 'will-less' in linguistic use supports the notion that the broader designation 'will' remains a measure of a potential capacity to perform a difficult (and often needed) task—for which some are less qualified than others. In this sense the term itself is value-suggestive—a willingness to take on a task, the accomplishment of which being the actual measure of the effort's value. Thus, 'will'—as presently used—no longer identifies a faculty, and so circumvents its older traditions of psychological use. It is now a normative designation, subject to the value of the action it generates. We are all willing or unwilling—as our needs match the case as it unfolds.

Of course, the most heart-felt and fervently pursued endeavor is not always successful—but no fault of yours, my friend; you gave it your best shot—we expect you for dinner on Saturday. This is the democratic way of looking at such intentional acts as "willing." In totalitarian regimes, however, the concept of "objective guilt" shows up. In this context, there is no question of intent—success or failure is the only measure. Here, willingness—an individual virtue—is measured differently when it results in a failure to satisfy the collective, material, demand. A failed willingness then shares equal guilt (and punishment) with the failure interpreted as a consequence of unwillingness.

III

THE GIVEN

I SAY THERE IS no given that is pristine in its location—unaffected by any priors—from which all else follows. The sober-sides say otherwise. They insist that—whether polychrome or plain, forthrightly sharp or oblique/obscure—it doesn't matter what you do, as long as the particulars you engage all emerge from the nature of the first given—its true nature, mind you, none of that whiney-feely stuff. The given, they say, is always there—fully formed—right there for all of us—and even you—if only you would look back far enough, and think ahead to listen.

So get up on your feet, my boy! Stand straight! Don't totter! See the difference? The given real appears when we are ready; it is in clear focus and shines bright upon the consecutive coherences of its own created world. The given is at one with flux. It's up to these-days citizens (teachers, preachers, and other such) who do not stray, but build their subjects out from within the always given—to determine what is both here and there and everywhere—for us to recognize. But such determinations, from time to time, create a lot of controversy and, sometimes, bloodshed.

To all this, I can say nothing, whether from my front or back—for I am equally straight and crooked in all my parts—neither of which were given me—I just liked the way each looked, and took them up in passing. They seem to get along. I can skip or totter as is appropriate for different settings—although I can no longer do a handstand or reach straight-leg below my toes. For dallying, I prefer a 'who' to a 'what.' A 'what' can be given back—full refund—no questions asked. But have you ever tried to return a 'who?' To whom, I ask, would you give back a 'who' to? Returning a 'what' is somewhat easier—you can give one to a similar other. Unlike a 'who,' a

THE GIVEN

'what' can be gregarious: They'll talk your ear off, and want the highest off the hog for dinner—but they don't care who dies before their time is due.

If you want to know: It's true: I deeply disbelieve in givens—but I can't let it out just yet. Every 'who' and 'what' I know would feel betrayed. So, to explicate:

The given, if at all, is everywhere.
It is in the moss that lives under deadfall in the winter woods—
in weeds that gather sunlight onto idle boulders in the fields of summer.
The given sounds the anguished clang of making stubborn metal into art.
It smells the spray that firms a coif when dying first appears.
It celebrates the discards that live their span in others' garbage.

When priapic, a given will praise paintings of reluctant nudes.
Rejected, it tut-tuts the central cities, now beyond recall—
places made empty-gray and impotent by lies and degradation.
When aesthetic, givens extol the cosmic ambition of a square—
the one that preens as art—although it sits within a larger square.
Givens commend the high-taste acumen of metal boxes
that stretch a ware-house length in rural Texas,
and smile at painted splashes on the best of Belgian linen.

But despite all caveats—the given remains the ground, the Grundlage, from which all else must grow. It is the unmediated beginning—the prime unmoved mover—the reason that creates its reasoning—the big-bang—the first sentence of the story. You have not lived until you find (or make) a given.

Without a given nothing follows—the given contains the scheme for what it means to follow. Later on, it shows forth what there is that follows it. Great edifices are built on proper givens—be they castles on granite cliffs or smart money hidden in the Cayman Islands. But, if we go back far enough (few now want to) there is only one given (can't you see it?)—the primordial glimmer in the Heavens that announces (without doubt) the beginning of what we are.

From another vantage, the given is the end—the multiples of "which" that becomes the singular of the "where" we must all arrive at. Without a given, there is no "must." But to embrace a "must" (foolish boy) we must ask (demand) that it explain the consequences of all that has been given—all that we must follow to arrive at the where (and what) we are. Argue but obey, I say.

In this second sense, the given is the final cause—the coalescence—the reason for it all—the purpose of beginning. This given is that to which the first cause is directed by the giver who exists before the first given becomes the prototype of further action.

Yet such givens, whether first or final, are different from each other every time we re-think the nature of their givers—and the source of their authority. For millennia, a Creator—benign or otherwise—has been the eternal source of all that follows. But philosophy (even before Christ) becomes the spoiler by questioning the autonomy of the given that would precede and authorize, the edicts it supports. Philosophical spoilage continues by questioning the refutation, asserted by that (first) given, that it has no need (one that any series logically has) to require a prior giver that gives it both being and authority. Here on middle earth—as we know—all parents need parents of their own to provide the impetus for our further reaches.

So all givens, whether first or final, seem to face a regress. Whether this is corrosive or supportive, is a matter of the belief that forms the given. Within the constraints of ordinary language, every given has a source—a "giver." In each particular case, then, the question arises: Who (what) is it that gives the given? Even Venus was sourced: She sprang from the head of Jove. (Would that I had been there to see her in her emerging prime). But there need not be takers in our little places for such a marvelous given. Venus, e.g., may be too scary. You and I had better settle for the girl next door—a given that we better understand.

But here in sober middle-earth, the given is serious stuff. Without a given we have little substance—we can neither be firemen without fires nor financiers without a deal. Yet, searching for one's given is seldom fun—especially when that given is not a consequence of birth or fortune—nor even of your best endeavors. When (on occasion) I remain aloof during the festivities of the righteous, and dismiss the givens there insisted on, someone will be sure to accuse me of distorting what is truly for the taking, by exercising the deviant preferences of my pre-festive longings—such as for the parson's many daughters. But not to worry—I no longer have fantasies of autonomous power: (Get thee behind me, Charity—or did I favor her older sister Grace? Hope is still too young to be a player).

Those who dote on givens—the jowly smiley well-fed folk in the castles on the hill—they hold firm to the givens they have taken. They understand

THE GIVEN

it as their due. To the milling herd of gazelles and wildebeests below, they say: We both derive from the Big Given—and that gives us good reason for our taking. As you will learn, giving and taking make up both our givens. (As they say: We all come from the same Giver). You must understand that a given is made actual by its takers (us)—and its givers (you). Without you, there would be no us—and that would be a shame. So, my dears (however unkempt and ill-mannered you may be)—don't be jealous of the other side. Try to do what (if we had to) we would gladly do for you: Give more of yourselves: Pray; donate to worthy causes; buy and spend to keep up with changing tastes; and cheerfully pay the going interest rates. Your best efforts will assure the trickle-down that will help you clean the kitchen floor in your later years.

This appeal is in the curriculum of every school devoted to the pedagogy of give-and-take. Spelled out, it teaches how to avoid the discomforts (spasms of conscience about third-world poverty, fears of global warming, abhorrence of the prevalence of aids in Africa, queasiness about Los Angeles couplings, and uneasiness about money-laundering in Manhattan)—such discomforts that, if acted upon, would be harmful to those who have both the giving and the taking gene. To take a given requires belief. Unbelievers—beware of takers who pretend that they are also givers!

Yet, givens can often be benign—especially when they are requisites for games. Serious games, such as logical systems, locate their givens in their primitive operators and rules of formation. When these games function syntactically (internally) the givens are rules that define the system and distinguish it from other games with different rules and operators. As long as the derivative functions are consistent, the syntactic givens define the game as a tautology: Reference is to the rules by which it plays—and to the plays the rules permit.

When the reference function of a system extends to the physical world, however, questions arise as to the nature (knowability) of the rule referred to. What then is or is not given? As the semantics of a system presumes to say something about (external) entities—the saying becomes a proposition that takes on the task (risk) of extending the truth function from the system's internal workings (coherence)—to a posit of correspondence between what is said and some part of the world. This posit—or proposition—can range from the evident to the speculative—but once made, the proposition itself becomes part of our attempt to understand the the world.

To show this, I offer the familiar example of a purportedly self-evident proposition: "The cat is on the mat." Questions and answers then begin: "When?—Now!" " When is now?—When I said it!" "When was that?—Just before!" The inquiry continues: "Is it a cat or a cat-like dog—or (as in the children's story) a rat-in-disguise?" "It isn't clear to me—as I wasn't close enough to see." "Is the mat a worn blanket—or grandma's old fur coat?" "It could have been either—for all I know." And so the story goes.

I offer another familiar example—fashioned to look into the cosmos for the elementary utterance (protocol sentence) upon which a truly empirical language is built: "Red spot here now." (Josef Albers would ask his classes at the Yale Art School to bring in an example of the "greenest green." The offerings ranged from tan to blue. None won—although the vocabulary to account for the differences expanded.) But going back to our basics: "Which spot are you referring to?" "Why that one—the one I'm (now) pointing at!" "Is the spot the one that is more purple-red or more red-orange?" "I don't know—but it's the spot to which I was pointing." Does language then, need to be ostensive to complete its referential meaning? Or is "indubitable reference" only an anthropological theory that traces the development between the first given: gesture—and the associated sounds that then—in our species—evolve into language?

We can watch the early film (black and white and somewhat worn) made in the the 1920's, of the philosopher who first uttered "red spot here now"—hoping thereby to demonstrate the seamlessness between language and reality, by first reducing language to that immediate utterance (the seamless conjunction between word and world) and then assuming that the internal givens of logic would extend it to a full panoply of sensible discourse—thereby giving us an adequate way to know—not merely describe the limits of the real world. This would keep the non-empirically-minded talk—all that speculative, visionary, sceptical, confessional, fictional, poetic, stuff—out of our utterances, and unwelcome in our minds.

But the world—before and after our times of living—is in constant flux (from our vantage—an irrefutable given). So, too, are the languages used through the millennia to describe the changes in the assaultive flow of clashing givens (itself a historically irrefutable given). But linguistic reference to the world, once made, becomes a part of the world—and so contributes to the changes that question the limits of any assertion of a given.

There are however, recreational games requiring givens (facsimiles of the real stuff) that are as precise—but not as portentous as the ones that

THE GIVEN

count for acquiring empirical truths. If, e.g., I move a bishop in a way that is rule-specific for a knight, I may not be adhering to the rules of chess—but I need not be wrong about the rest of the world. Who knows what my motives are? Even I may not know. They could be about rattling my opponent or, perhaps, inventing the new game of "Schuss." What I did was to offer a new given which—considering the standardized rules (givens) of chess—will not be incorporated into that game. The choice I offer is not an imperative that threatens life or portends chaos—but it might produce a different game.

With these observations, I have come a way to distinguishing between a transcendent given that is there for belief through it's claim to eternality, and one that we—its time-bound progeny—devise as a starting point for our better knowing of the world. The first must have an otherworldly source to defend it against the caveats—the demands for proof—leveled by the second. But the latter, in turn, needs to acknowledge that, with its empirical formulations and their limits, there is much of consequence—mortality as inevitable, meaning as a fluctuating interim, and the changing historical residues of memory—that it cannot completely address.

IV

GIVING

Before the given one begins with,
there is silence.
The giver of a given is usually hidden
from those who get the goods.

It would be easier for a given
to start all by itself—without
a giver who might want
due recognition—
after all the giving is finished
being given.

What comes next is
ascertained by following
other rules that govern givens:
To seek a giver, once a given
is in place,
risks a corrosive regress
to a prior given
that also shields its giver—
and so stretches patience
in the longer run.

GIVING

Or—if one so believes—
a first un-given can be found
to which the giver gives the rule
to make the notion of
a given what it is.

Then it follows (doesn't it?) that the
"first ungiven given,"
a concoction of the Greeks,
must be a blood relation of the
"prime unmoved mover."
Or is that a sin?

Aristotle didn't think so—
because he knew
both types of blood are fine.
But Aquinas thought so—
because, for all the similarity,
he had a different blood
in mind.

V

TAKING

To give—To take
These are infinitives—also infinities—
for they co-exit in both language and eternity.
I say "The Given" when I don't know what precedes it—
whether God, or nothing, or the same old thing.

And I say "A Taking" when
the plot of land I worked so hard to get
was called by them an aquifer,
and confiscated for the common good—
until the condominium could be built
upon my bit of privileged ground.

Miss Given is a package to behold unless
misgiven—when taken to a fat old Prince
where she would have to stoop while waiting
for the taking—when instead—

she should rightly and for the best part
be unwrapped—unfettered and
straightened up—by namely me.
She then could sway away—
fall soft across my bony lap—
within extended reach of
my oh-so-patient hands.

VI

ERLEBS AND QUALIA

Some philosophies adopt a strategy whose aim is to arrive at—or "construct"—an elementary given from which further, more complex, constructions can be derived. The examples I comment on here, are Rudolph Carnap's "Logische Aufbau der Welt" of 1928, and Nelson Goodman's "Structures of Appearance" of 1951. These are both logical systems whose elements are not representations of the world, but serve to analyze the proper development of object languages—which contain true statements about the world. The aim is to find a basic given through a reduction. In Carnap's work these elements are called "Erlebs" or minimal time-slices that together constitute a concrete experience. In Goodman' work, the elements are more elementary and abstract—"qualia" of time, place, color, which when combined together result in a "concretum"—a first element of sensory experience. By using various logical procedures, these primitives are elaborated into more complex constructions that act as analogues to (codifications of) the epistemic methods we actually use.

Both systems are solipsistic, for they begin with the analysis of individual experience. With Carnap, the system is also realistic: Each erleb, as it is offered as a least-perceptible slice of individual experience, is minimally real. With Goodman, the system is nominalistic—each quale is an abstraction prior to its joining with the other two quales, at which point it becomes a concretum—equally real—but larger in scope—given the varying equivalences of the "time" quale with the others—than is Carnap's "Erleb." An Erleb's moment is minimal—a single time of smallest slicing. Goodman's concretum is more generous. By making time a quale—correlative with place and color—his system is open to larger dimensions of interpretation.

We note that that Carnap does not push his Erlebs beyond the limits of the sensate. However artificial these time-slices may seem, they begin with the actual–minimal, and then face the difficulties of linkage—of construction into a coherent experience. Goodman, however, is willing to begin with hypotheticals: Quales occur prior to experience. They are abstract in the sense that different configurations occur at different times, in different place, and with different appearances. Goodman's construction, then, does not begin with a given minimal perception. Rather, it provides, a-priori, the initial units out of which such experience do begin.

For a committed empiricist, Goodman's form of rationalism would seem difficult to accept. For a skeptical empiricist, Carnap's minimal-percepts might seem artificial. But as both constructions (Carnap's and Goodman's) come out of individual experience, their worlds begin within an individual consciousness. They are solipsistic in that they are prior to—but at some point in the construction—must engage with other minds. In a non-mystical context, this means that, in their elaboration, they must be (able to be) translated and incorporated into scientific method—the parameters of which are not individual but communal. We note also that the systems referred to are both phenomenal—they describe how our individual sensory perceptions are built into experiences—however much these constructions are themselves conceptual.

Of course, neither system provides a "picture" (a sensory reality) of a foundational basis. These constructions, rather, can better be understood as methodological—as a basis for logical thought rather than as a minimal sensory basis of phenomenal experience. Their purpose, then, is hortatory—as instructions (and admonitions) for separating actual sense from inventive nonsense. Yet, in practice, both turn out to be incomplete. They cannot (as yet) be logically translated into physical systems of the various sciences—which have their own primitives, e.g., atomic particles, neurons, etc. on which to base their descriptions of the world. They each have their full-fleshed languages that require constant re-examination but not reduction. As the sciences are the experimentally supported source of what we come (empirically) to know—and the systems considered here are hypothetical constructions about how (sensory) experience occurs, combines, and develops into the data describing an objective world—the transition between the two is quite difficult—as has been the case.

In effect, such a transition (between the phenomenal and the physical) would entail a logical progression from the elements or primitives chosen for the individual construction, to the propositions of scientific language. This is a somewhat Kantian move—one that distinguishes philosophy from science: Philosophy does not provide truths about the world—science does. Philosophy asks, rather, how science can do this, and answers by analyzing the perceptual, categorical, and developmental bases of veridical thinking. This is the question in all of Kant's work: How is knowledge possible? It is the critical question in each of his "Critiques." Each particular answer (physical sciences, ethics, aesthetics) purports to tell us how we can know what we seek, by identifying the relevant units of experience, and then by plotting the logic of their combinations into the actual ingredients of a given form of knowledge. In the Critique of Pure Reason, the units are the "non-reducible" elements of physical reality—and the question is how their aggregates can be described as forms of empirical knowledge. In the Critique of Practical Reason, the procedure is reversed and the question—the categorical demand—is that our individual actions conform to a rule that "should" govern everyone's action in like circumstances. In the Critique of Judgment, Kant retreats somewhat and asks that we put aside our individual ambitions and preferences so that we may sense (disinterestedly) the beauty—the "harmony"—of creation, and use it as a model for the super-sensible "completeness" of the sensible..

The systems we are considering here—Carnap's and Goodman's—have a common historical identity. They are both based on the assumption that it is individual experience upon which one builds to erect a proper foundation for scientific knowledge. This returns us to Descartes and the cogito—the building of God and the Universe from the "unassailable" proof of existence through the fact that I think—and, ergo, that I am a thinking thing. Upon this first surety, I can (by further examination of my thoughts) build to the existence and attributes of God, and to the actualities of the physical world.

I believe that there is a historical Romanticism involved in this (solipsistic) search for a basis. It is derived from the philosophical primacy of individual experience as the basis for understanding life—a thesis which has in common the soul-searching of the earlier periods of existential primacy—the Hegelian pilgrimage of spirit; Kierkegaard's insistence on subjective authenticity for individual belief; and, more dubiously, Nietzsche's image of Zarathustra's laughter. These all have a solipsistic base, and build their worlds from the elementary images of the world as individually perceived and then generated into a collectivity. This prizing of a romantic or speculative source of any construction that is at all truth generative—be it in philosophy or art—is a thesis that Carnap, undoubtedly, would have strongly rejected. Goodman might have been more sympathetic—as he was quite interested in art.

Carnap later gave up on the search for an intersection between the logics of the phenomenal and physical realms, and turned his analytic powers to problems in the physical domain. The physical-scientific answer to the question of "what there is" would now rest on the hypothesis-experiment-confirmation procedures of scientific method—not in a reduction to primitives of explanation. It became apparent that scientific hypotheses do not depend on a common reduction to a phenomenal base—the efficacy in generating experimental confirmation of particular hypotheses about the physical realm is sufficient. Nor do descriptions in the separate sciences require a reduction to a single basis within science (the language, e.g., of physics as being more fundamental than that of Biology) for the construction of their epistemic worlds.

Goodman, perhaps because of his interest in art, did not think the distinction between domains—whether they have a realistic or phenomenalistic base—whether actual or fictional—to be either clear or defeating. He pursued avenues of interchange between logic and art in his later books: "Languages of Art," and "Fact, Fiction, and Forecast."

The difference in ways the factor of "time" is treated in these theories is important for other parts of my discussion. Carnap's primitive, "Erleb," occurs in a minimal moment of perception, while Goodman's "time-quale" is congruent, past or future, with the other quales—place and color—that form a concretum. This distinction can also be found in the contrast between Wittgenstein's "picture theory" of language, with its immediate configuration of "atomic facts," and his later turn to the notion that language is a "game"—where the world is understood through changes in forms and contexts of reference.

The distinction between immediate perception and the relativities of memory and dream, occurs as a "Leitmotif" in my later chapters—particularly in the contrast I propose between "actual" and "real" in conceptions of the world and self—and from that, into my discussion of God, immortality, death and after-life.

VII

WITTGENSTEIN AND SILENCE

THERE ARE TIMES WHEN, and places where, Philosophy ends. The stories then told reflectively exhaust the mechanisms of what philosophers can say—and with a nod of resignation (or completion—or exhaustion) indicate why, after their last words, nothing further can—or should—be said. We then enter the realm of (philosophically) necessary silence.

Ludwig Wittgenstein ends his Tractatus-Logico-Philosophicus (1922) with the statement "Wovon man nicht sprechen kann, darüber muss man schweigen." (It also appears in his preface.) This is possibly the most famous statement in modern philosophy. My translation, which differs somewhat from extant ones, is: " Of what one cannot speak, about that one must be silent." The version by Pears and McGuinness (1971 Tr.) is: "What we cannot speak about we must pass over in silence." The differences, for me are important. The first is that in my version there are two references—wovon (of what) and darüber (about that). In the translation noted, there is only one—(what . . . about). A second difference is the one between the admonition to "be silent" and the other to "pass over in silence." This second can be dramatized as the difference between "shut up" and "abstain from speaking."

I suggest that these differences promote a reading of Wittgenstein's thesis that reveals a rift—between what he hopes can be established as "what is the case" i.e., atomic facts and their developments—and what must be left outside, i.e., "thinking (but not articulating) what should-not be thought." The "wovon" is an indeterminate reference—that of which we cannot speak. The "darüber" is an admonition—to not speak of that which cannot (sensibly) be spoken of. There is no suggestion here that the unspeakable does not exist—but rather—that it evades a parsing into atomic facts. In the preface Wittgenstein also states: "The aim of the book is to draw a limit . . . not to thought but to the expression of thoughts, for in order to draw a limit to thought, we should have to find both sides of the limit thinkable." If the experienced world were the logical world—the complete aggregate of atomic facts—then the unspeakable would not exist. But such completeness is nonsense—as much so as saying what cannot be thought. This admonition becomes clearer when we translate "cannot" into "should-not." Wittgenstein's hope was for a rational world—with the "unsinnlich" aspects falling away as we climb his ladder. "Should–not" is the better way to give reason for the climb.

Here, I suggest an elaboration of W's last sentence which gives my bearing on its meaning:

"Wovon man nicht sprechen kann, davon kann man noch denken. Aber darüber, muss man schweigen."

I translate this as: "Of what one cannot speak, of that one can still think, but about that one must be silent."

I take the three prefix's: "Wovon," "Davon," Darüber," to successively delimit the field of reference. "Wovon" is everything there is—actual-virtual, past-future, factual-fictional, necessary-impossible. "Davon" is everything that can be thought—that content, limited by time and capacity, that there is to think about. Daruber, the smallest of the three, is that which an acquiescence to the limits of the sensible prohibits one from speaking of.

The hope embedded here, is that the ladder of ascent—the historical habit of speaking non-sense, successively rectified—will eliminate its metaphysical propensity for error, and allow the eventual (and when is that?) rejection of the scaffolding that brings one to that place of semantic clarity—an elaboration of existence from the base of "atomic facts." Once there, one finds desirable company: "The totality of facts in logical space—is the world. (1.13)" "A logical picture of facts is a thought.(3)" "The totality of true thoughts is a picture of the world (3.01)." "In order to tell whether a picture is true or false—we must compare it with reality. (2.223)." These statements indicate a progression—from what is the case, to how we know what is the case, and to how we verify (by comparison) that our picture of reality is, in fact, true (or false): "A picture has logico-pictorial form in common with what it depicts. (2.2)." Now if the picture, as so compared, is indeed false, this form does not conform to the totality of facts. Then we must be silent—not commit to sense what is pictured—and reject images which, in truth, are false. But all pictures show their sense—even if such sense misrepresents the facts it pictures—or shows "pseudo-facts"—thereby misrepresenting the world. Early on, however, Wittgenstein makes a statement that modifies the strictness of his division: "If I can imagine objects combined in states of affairs, I cannot imagine them excluded from the possibility of such combinations (2.0121." But such possibilities occur—are central to—the visual arts and literature. It would seem, then, that one can countenance fictional as well as actual worlds. In this way, the admonition to "be silent" is weakened, or, at least, relegated to only some contexts of thought.

A consideration of some aesthetic issues might be helpful here.

The term "picturing" needs elaboration—for it is the dividing line between what can be thought and (the limits on) what should be said. Wittgenstein's claim that languages are "logical pictures" of reality—that they show what they state—could give us a way of approaching the difficult problem he poses: How a tautologous system of logic can have any bearing (reference, interpretation, description, clarification, etc.) on what we know about the world. What kind of picture, then? Is such picturing true of all languages—or all variants of a language? Evidently, there are no generic notions of picturing at issue here—there are too many differences in historical styles of representation or, more strongly, verisimilitude. But neither is there a generic notion of "language pictures"—for no one knows all languages. But the commonality between these, as Wittgenstein says, is that language-as-picture completely states what it shows—although the image (content) shown may not be factually true: "What a picture represents, it represents independently of its truth or falsity, by means of its pictorial form. (2.22). But how do we distinguish between true and false pictorial form? There are, after all, many conventions of "picturing."

When one knows a language, one cannot not know what is being said by another speaker of that language. This is an empirical—not a logical assertion. Yes, there are many conditions—audibility, dialect, coherence, etc.—that play a part. But given satisfaction of these conditions, we immediately "understand" what is being said to us. No interpretation or analysis is required. In the same sense, when we see a picture, we immediately see what is being represented—no extrapolation from marks to images is required. Here, too, certain conditions—familiarity with medium and style, etc.—are necessary. But given satisfaction of these, we also [cannot–not see] what a picture represents. But, then, we cannot completely (or even cumulatively) understand what a statement "means" or what a picture "shows." Further, we cannot know—merely from a representation—(even a "logical" one)—whether the representation is true or false.

During expeditions in the late 19th and early 20th centuries, when anthropologists showed photographs to primitive peoples in the South American jungles—photographs taken of those very people—the response was bewilderment. They did not see representations—only grey smudges.

George Catlin, a 19th century American painter, journeyed to Indian territories in the Western plains—hoping to record the native people. He carried with him his painting gear, and gifts—tools, clothing, and jewelry—with which to persuade tribe members to pose for him. Catlin must have had an ingratiating way—for the Indians posed willingly, took the presents gladly, and showed little hostility. But although they could see the paintings as representations, they took little interest—for these pictures had neither spiritual nor practical value. So Catlin returned back East with the paintings he had made—an early record of an indigenous civilization that used different symbol systems to inform their lives.

Titian, the great Venetian Renaissance artist, did his early work influenced by the Florentine "classical" method—notably of Michelangelo and Raphael—which emphasizes clear linear contours and systematic perspective in the compositions. But Titian's interest in light and color as compositional determinants, led him eventually to abandon the Florentine dictates in favor of such values as emergence, density, luminosity. This contrast became generalized and is (to this day) called the battle between "disegno e colore." Vasari, the notable art-critic and contemporary of Titian, when looking at the late paintings said (as is reported) that he saw nothing much but free-floating light and color—to the detriment of clarity of composition as well as to the sense (subject) of the paintings.

In late 20th century Modernism, there was much interest in the "end" of the artistic tradition. However historically and theoretically motivated this theory is, my focus here is on the symbolic theories that were used to "express" this eventuality. I suggest that two procedures—also formulated in analytic Philosophy—were at work here. These procedures are "reduction" and "regimentation." The first is a discarding of "superfluous, ambiguous, representational, decorative," elements in the artwork; the second is a formal ordering of the remaining (discovered) "essentials" within a compatible pictorial matrix. In the visual arts, Mondrian is a prime exemplar of this process—moving from traditional landscape to geometric abstraction. He gradually limited his pictorial means to vertical-horizontal oppositions and primary colors. For Mondrian, however, this passage was not an "endgame," but an optimistic and expanding opening to the future—an optimistic Modernism freed from the limitations of picturing. (A similar optimism can sometimes be found in the later Wittgenstein). Mondrian, in his last works, pushed past the geometric stability he had achieved into a search for the less architectonic value of pure rhythm, e.g., his "Broadway Boogie-Woogie" of 1942-3. Other artists of this and later times, while committed to the stylistic processes of "abstracting," were, however, also deeply involved with notions of finality (and despair). The painter Kasimir Malevich, in the 1930's, fled Communist Russia and its strictures on modern art, to settle in Germany and pursue a minimalist-abstract mode of painting. He had been deeply wounded by the Soviet effort to translate old academic art into new propagandist kitsch—and followed this experience into paintings that showed the theoretical—if not experiential—culmination of art into the minimal components still left unsullied. The "White on White"—a tilted white square on a just perceptively different white ground—is a case in point. But it is also a picture about which very little can be said—unless one uses a language of the exotic kind that Wittgenstein wants to dismiss from serious thought.

Other attacks on the continuity of pictorial language came from Dada and Surrealism. These were not counter theories—but imperatives of historical disobedience: An art that no longer needs its name. But this move was more an attack on customs of appreciation than on the verities of art-making. Duchamp's "R-Mutt"—a commercial urinal exhibited in an art museum—shows the thrust of this critique. It is directed against "aesthetic sensibility"—and the implication is that anything suitably authenticated—as by being exhibited in galleries and museums—has properties that then become (can be appreciated as) aesthetic properties: "Anything is art if it functions in the domain of art"—and correspondingly—"aesthetic properties are those that objects have when exhibited as art." Is there a circularity here? Not to worry: (If so, then so, so then, not if—but if so, then not so).

Wittgenstein answers the question "how is logic possible?" with the answer that without logic, there would be no question. Logic is a-priori. Its reality is prior to our experience of (the facts of) the world—rather, it is the basis for (a human form of) the experience of knowing facts. But there is illogic—images without corresponding facts—that also is a human form of experience. Wittgenstein holds that il-logic gives us a false world. It gives us pseudo-facts which do not picture things—or, instead, gives us pictures which do not correspond to the facts of things—the (totality of) things that are (constitute) the world. But facts are things logically represented by language—actual things are (exist) independent (ly) of our representations. Our representing ends with us—when we die. Things continue on. Living, we formulate true facts and false (pseudo) facts—both of which—as formulations—exist in reality. There can be illogical representations (pictures) of the world when (true) facts no longer show the world in any useful way. This way illogic becomes meaningful—and can be "pictured"—represented as a fact. As such, it is often useful.

The "end of art" is a consequence of—an artistic answer to—such an eventuality. This notion extolls, instead of (pictorial) logic, the power of meaninglessness: Automatic writing—nonsense-language (speaking in tongues)—infatuation with the anti-reference of chance and accident—the ubiquity of concrete and aleatory music—pure (preferably pre-reasoned) gesture—exhibitions of residues of accidental inattention—trophies of boredom. These are all artistic responses—historically called Dada (itself a nonsense syllable)—to the 20th century disillusionment with logic, progress, meaning—all those failed enlightenment values—the reactions against which followed both world wars in the 20th century. Yet this was also the time of the "correctives" of analytic philosophy, and of Wittgenstein's major writings.

One further intersection with art: Picasso's "Portrait of Kahnweiler" (1910), is a major work of Analytic Cubism. I t is constructed with modular transparent elements whose intersections unite figure with picture plane. The spatial structure, although not uniform, becomes continuous throughout. A delicate balance is maintained between continuity and concretion—this by means of relative densities and representational remnants—signifiers that refer in passing to the "given" object-space distinction before analysis. "Kahnweiler" is still there, but has become part of—continuous with—the space he inhabits. Then an aesthetic change occurs—indeed, an opposition to all the clarity unity and tidiness of analysis: Picasso's "Suze." (1912). This is the name of a then popular soft drink in Paris. One time (probably when Braque wasn't around) Picasso took off the label from a bottle of "Suze," and glued it onto a canvas—which also contained painted Cubist elements. The move marked the advent of Synthetic Cubism. This was more than a visual shock—it was a theoretical undermining of continuity and consistency—the extant earmarks of pictorial virtue. A different world—tacky, trivial, commercial, and coarse—entered into the pristine modular unity of the old. This was an uneasy cohabitation—a kind of class warfare in which neither inhabitant would relinquish properties so as to allow the construction of another unity—a classically true synthesis. With this physically modest but theoretically powerful gesture, Picasso gave pictorial permission for incursion, intrusion, uncivility. Discontinuity and the logic of illogic became accepted procedures in the making of art. Picasso's own prolific and diverse output shows he didn't much care about distinctions—except as reasons to create even more.

The analogy I offer is between the aesthetic move between Analytic and Synthetic Cubism, and Wittgenstein's philosophical move from Language-as-Picture to Language-as-Game. It is not (cannot be) a precise analogy: The term "between" refers to the creation of a new artistic style—but the old remains happily with us. The term "from," however, refers to a superseding—a replacement of one theory by another. Change occurs for different reasons in philosophy and art: In philosophy, theories become inadequate—and are rejected; in art, styles are exhausted, and are then venerated.

Wittgenstein (to my mind) had an inordinate faith in basing his "Language as Picture" thesis—even in principle—on a world that is construed as "the totality of facts." There are evident problems with this: How could one ever know such a world? Is this "totality" itself a fact? How is the totality of facts different from the totality of thoughts? Does every fact have its object? Additionally—the effort to base linguistic knowing on the model of pictorial representation—seems a confabulation of terms. The truth or falsity of pictured images seems to me both aesthetically and historically irrelevant. The attempt to ascertain pictorial truth—be it logically or imagistically offered—is more an invitation to a critical journey through successive cultural histories—into the plethora of picturing, starting with the first cave-paintings—where language was probably more rudimentary than was drawing. How, then, has it happened that "picturing" is offered as a determinant that shows—from all made—which linguistic utterances are ("eternally") true of the world? It would seem that more critical journeys are in order. Wittgenstein calls his notion of picturing a "comparison with reality." True—if understanding what the picture shows, is also understanding the world as the picture shows it. To say, however, that a picture can be true (represents "facts") is a different claim—which cannot be answered because of the historicity of picturing. It can, however, be linguistically answered through first presenting a logically unified field from which the axioms of fact-telling can be then derived and (without contradiction) relegated to the subsequent (true) apprehension of a lived reality.

This concept, if taken historically, is reminiscently Hegelian—as it smacks of teleology. But Wittgenstein evidently would not countenance a merely historical scheme of "progress" to underlay his journey into a more knowable (and true) reality. He wanted knowledge to, in fact, be true—now. Indeed, he would probably have thought Hegel's view of history to be unfounded nonsense—the worst kind of metaphysical imposition on logical thought. But I don't know that. Indeed, Hegel does have his detractors among logicians—yet Wittgenstein does advise us to climb his own ladder—and then kick it away. He is after (has faith in the eventual achievability of) transparent windows between logic, language, and reality. It is the dominant philosophical theme of the Tractatus.

This direction of theorizing, however, can take us into the question of language acquisition—a question that Wittgenstein would put aside as one for the behavioral sciences—not philosophy. Yet, that approach to the conundrum of what "picturing" comes to—in the empirical (behavioral) sense—might very well afford another answer to Wittgenstein's call to silence.

At birth (our first entrance into the world) we are confronted by images and sounds. Gradually, these come together as mutual reference—first through ostension, a pointing to the subject of the sound made, then through the sound's (word's) reference to images of memory, anticipation, and desire. These words give images sequence and identity—a "stands—for" interaction occurs—between sounds and references—which is first mimicked and then continues to change (we can say "develops") throughout our sentient lives. The syntax, semantics and aggregate of words (language) also change (one could say "develops") throughout historical time. Evidently, the picturing of language changes correspondingly. This reciprocation, given the human capacity for memory and abstraction, constitutes thought and reference: we can think things that are not present, and refer to things we have not seen. We can then tell stories about all these—make pictures of them—and then develop ways of ascertaining which of these are "true."

So the thesis of "language as picture"" is not to suggest that language is a "picture of a thought"—but rather to assert a reciprocal transparency—between times—of what we say about our experienced world and its reality. But the reality of the world changes with our cultural—and its historical—sequence of experiences. So the "sensible" basis of our utterances must change as well—as does what can and cannot be said.

Wittgenstein states that the world is composed of facts not of things. It is often said that the history of science is a history of error. Facts are fungible. Things are what they are—whether we know them or not. The history of facts is a climbing of Wittgenstein's ladder. At every point there is some fact that loses sense and must be discarded—at every point, new facts emerge and are incorporated into knowledge. Some choose not to speak of discarded facts—others gleefully take them on, refurbish them, and incorporate them into the fictions of art, metaphysics, ethics, politics, and religion. It can be difficult to discard obsolete but seductive facts. Depending on their form of "non-sense," some might remain useful, others pleasurable, still others—powerful. I think that Wittgenstein would agree—which is possibly why he also states in his preface: " . . . how little is achieved when these problems are solved." There is also that admonition at the end—perhaps no more than an idealistic hope for closure—to "throw away the ladder after one has climbed up on it." But why throw it away? The errors (if they are such) of the past are not disreputable. They are efforts to know—which have their own specific charms—and they also warn that error making is not over. In the transition between the Tractatus and the Philosophical Investigations, we see that Wittgenstein took this very much to heart.

Much of the "Tractatus" is devoted to showing how logic—whose propositions are themselves tautological—can be used as a "scaffolding" for our better understanding of the world—in effect, a clarification of how our thoughts, logically refined, can be molded into empirically true propositions. That this is a task, rather than an accomplishment, is shown by Wittgenstein's metaphor of the ladder—which indicates the nature of the process—rung by rung—before we can kick away the ladder, remove the scaffolding which so far we have required, and live a rational life. (I have a caveat, here: I don't think that Wittgenstein ever thought this possible—only desirable—in a world better than he himself could hope for).

But to go on: As the "scaffolding" of the enterprise is largely logical analysis of ordinary language, the presumption arises that eventually we will have learned to speak correctly—are able to use language to picture our world as it is—so that our learned symbolizations that build on this, will be free of non-sense. A peaceable kingdom—for sure—but, as I say, an optimism that Wittgenstein could not himself share. The Tractatus is not a political treatise—for all its logic, it is more akin to theology. There is much left out—too much that does not fit into the purview of atomic facts and their elaboration—but remains a stubbornly persistent part of living. Wittgenstein threw barriers into the way of his own proposals, and realized their susceptibility to subversion by the inexpressible. He states (6.423): "Of the will as subject of the ethical, we cannot speak." And (6.522): "There is indeed the inexpressible. This shows itself; it is the mystical." For him, then, there is a realm of being that not only should not—but cannot—be said. It can be shown, however—through a picture, a fiction, through music, and in the utterances that poetically embrace sur-rationality. These, as one reading of the Tractatus indicates, are symbolic modes to be corrected, ignored, or waited out—as philosophy itself must be surmounted (6.54). This last is particularly distressing—for we have no guarantee that waiting will help. Further, we have conflicting reasons to believe that such surmounting would be desirable.

In the Philosophical Investigations (1953), Wittgenstein comes to reject the thesis in the Tractatus that there is a comprehensive logical structure underlying all propositions that "have sense." The "Investigations" is a scattered and somewhat aphoristic book—very different in form from the Tractatus—but one in which Wittgenstein also proposes a radically different thesis: Different forms of language are games that have their own rules—and what binds them all together as language (their inter-translatability) is a "family resemblance"—derived from a model of partial overlap—as in a tribe whose members disband to follow their separate needs but rejoin during festivals—so allowing the similarities and differences to be recognized and partially echoed throughout the total span, and variations, of the games being played.

This move, for me, speaks against the requirement of "sinnlich" (meaningful) upon which, in the Tractatus, Language is based. Although, in this later book, Wittgenstein does not indicate any capitulation to irrationality—as, e.g., that a language can be senseless and yet have an extra logical mode of meaning—but he does reject the picture theory (that a proposition shows what it says) for the more abstract notion of resemblance. This notion requires different rules for different languages, and it bases the inter-translatability between languages on similarities between the rules governing each game—similarities that permit different languages to be (if only partially) understood by all language speakers. This indicates that, although languages all have different layers of meaning—moving from the most logically explicit to the most poetically suggestive—they share a common structural basis. Even in the sciences, e.g., as in Psychology and Physics—while they are both after truth—their theories are expressed in different ways.

This returns us to the a-priori nature of the basic axioms of logical construction found in the Tractatus—the notion that without this common basis, the analysis of linguistic use and meaning would be impossible. But the newer "game" relationship between languages offered in the Investigations, indicates that within any given framework of linguistic use (as between different languages) no speaker will have the same range of comprehension across them all. (c.f., Quine's thesis of the "indeterminacy of translation"). Even within a (supposedly) single language, different rules apply: I remember the havoc wrought by "Finnegan's Wake" on classes in the English Novel—or the first bourgeois bewilderments when exposed to the lyrics of "Rap"—or to the sounds in Berg's "Lulu."

Given these differences, what then is the role (if any) of "silence" in this later thesis of "language as a game?"

In the Tractatus, Wittgenstein's call to silence is more than a directive—it is an admonishment, close to an imperative, that one "must" (more diffidently—"should") avoid speaking about the senseless. It was not that senselessness is without its pictures. Rather, it is that some language-pictures distort reality into irrational presentations—and these are not to be used when the goal (which all of us—should—share) is of speaking sense. The rationality of empirical science is the model of true descriptions of reality—granted. Even so, Wittgenstein does make numerous allusions, in the early work, to what must be left outside: "What the law of causality is meant to exclude cannot even be described" (T6.362). "It is clear that ethics cannot be put into words" (T6.421).

In the Investigations, such exclusions become a preference—a choice between relevant and aberrant games—and there is no consistent admonition to choose the one which pictures reality most accurately—the world does not go that way. With the change from "picture" to "game," the center (the reduction-to-logical-basis—the common denominator—the form of forms—the unmoved mover) is rejected. Instead, the philosophical approach to meaning becomes a parsing of indefinitely many "language games"—and of establishing (discovering?) the conditions that identify their family resemblances. Wittgenstein comes close here to what is called "Ordinary-Language" philosophy. But more importantly, he tries to reinterpret (and yet somehow maintain) the parameters that, in the Tractatus, are given as the scope and limits of "sensible" language. But the language-game proposal is too insistent, and its danger is that it can also be understood as extending to any sounds (utterances?) that some attenuated rule-like rule, will cover.

We can make-up reasons to cover whatever we formulate into a rule that underlies whatever game we make into a language. Is there nothing then—by dint, perhaps of "incoherence," or "opacity," or "unwarranted privilege"—that lies outside? If not, all utterance (even babble) can find its rule, and the roar and twitter of "non-sense" has no historical or formal reason to disappear.

In the Investigations, there is no call to silence, for the indefinite multiplicity of language-games implies that each is (sometimes) spoken and heard. But as each has its own rule—there being (now) no central standard or definition for a language—there is a buzzing in the sounds of speaking: Is what we hear an arcane syntax or is it just grunting? Does the very partiality of translation help the impetus to incoherence? To say: "Not in our life-time" is the optimistic answer. But when we look around—language, when it is used for unruly purposes, often reduces to babble. This, however, is a political consideration—a way to power.

To return again to the aesthetic: In the heydays of doctrinal worship of immediacy (Dada, Action Painting, Concrete Music), the distinction between language and babble—or screeching brakes- or speaking in tongues—or scratch and splash—was variously offered as a moral or an aesthetic replacement for the stale codifications of a suspect way of life. The distinctions made were usually between conformity and freedom. However this may play in the present—in those early halcyon days, rejecting the formalities marking the conservatives, while embracing the rarified emergence of irrationality, identified the Avant-Garde.

This historical replacement was aimed at the gap between feeling and manifestation—at the strictures that (purportedly) inhibit the translation of inner (private) emotion into outer (social) life—and artifacts. The resident culprits were logic and traditional style. But, paradoxically, these efforts at immediacy also came to show symptoms of indifference and anonymity. For a time this had its own appeal (every living thing—including you and me—an artist). Such appeals were buttressed by the inclusion of animal art and found objects within the arena of art-consideration (appreciation). But the various manifestations of "freedom" (an overdone truism) never jelled—that is, they never became (a true-transparency)—a "non-style" style. The efforts at reconstituting the world through its expressions have two main directions: First, from inner to outer—where the symptoms of feeling, in some or other context of belief are recognized—through artifacts or performance similes—as adequate representations of those feelings. Second: from outer to inner—where passing sights and random sounds are given rules of articulation and limit and are thus accepted as symbolic replicas of feeling events. Both these replacements (historically) are ephemeral—for their success depends upon agreement—a pact—between parties. The inner must find an outer for corroboration; the lower must find a higher for socialization. Neither can stand alone—in the sense that a language cannot survive if it is built on (or succumbs to) either affective (expressive)—or semantic (referential)—detachment from its "speakers-in-the-world."

My remarks here aim at projecting Wittgenstein's theory of "language as game" into arenas of usage. What constitutes an acceptable language—and what are acceptable differences between languages? The stipulation, in the Tractatus, is one of formal (both syntactic and semantic) coherence between languages. This describes a sufficiency between "states of affairs" and their linguistic transcription as "true propositions." But Wittgenstein's later denial, in the Investigations, that there can be an axiomatic reduction to a single (a-priori) basis for all languages—one which transfers the notion of language from universal form to the individual user—does not support the earlier claim. The hope in the Tractatus is that logical analysis shows me what I was not (fully) aware of—the possibility of a veridical transformation of experience into language. But in the Investigations, we are left wondering how far we can stretch this hope.

The social interchange between human languages may often be fuzzy—but it does not pose such problems—conviviality and a glass of wine are important for translation. What does pose a problem is Wittgenstein's strictures, in the Tractatus, on what can be said—what is logically acceptable as true and verifiable—and his optimistic scenario that we can climb past—discard all illogic—and then live happily with what is left. This thesis, as articulated, is as beautiful as a Mondrian painting. But it is not a prescription for the future. It is, as I suspect, an unwitting participation in Hegel's insistence on Spirit's march to self-purification. There is no good reason within the ongoing communities of speakers, why languages would be better served by any such reduction. And there is no evidence that such discipline would improve the welfare of human kind. I think that Wittgenstein came to see this—and was thereby influenced, in the Investigations, to abandon his picture-theory of language for the theory that is destructive to his earlier ambitions—a theory of language as a game played to satisfy the variety of its users needs. Wittgenstein's acknowledgment of the "unspeakable," is coupled with his dismay at contemporary attacks on the common basis of rational systems—such as Godel's thesis that mathematics, if taken as a deductive system, shows that inconsistency is inherent between the methodologies of different proofs—and that this denies the possibility of an ultimate reduction to a single unified basis—even for mathematics! (A.W. Levi—"Wittgenstein, the Man and his Philosophy"—1967) This thesis could have influenced Wittgenstein's later denial, in the Philosophical Investigations, that there is a (single) logical basis applicable to referential language so as to validate (and rehabilitate) our varying utterances about the world. (I discuss this further in the following chapter). The recognition of this disjunction between the tautology of logical propositions, the meanings looked for in metaphysical propositions, and the "truth" of physical descriptions, suggests that Wittgenstein—in the most salutary way—is a "cusp" figure—one who tried to bridge the older substance of speculative language and the newer methods of logical analysis. His aim was to clarify (decontaminate) the language of such speculation through analysis. What he came to realize (as I believe) is that language, so clarified, does not serve the purposes of the larger array of language users. On both a social and private level, this was important, and probably painful to him—but the recognition marks his greatness as a philosopher.

VIII

COMPARISONS—CONSTRAINTS

1} Tautology → Logic; Pleonism → Persuasion
    Forms of Identity → Sameness (strong); Repetition (weak)
        (Sameness → contextual; Repetition → habitual)
    Forms of Difference → Heterology (strong); Discord (weak)
        (Heterology → systematic contrast; Discord → social conflict)

2} Form & Content;
    Form → consistency or inconsistency; Content → Sense or Non-Sense

3} First Cause, Formal cause, Material cause, Final Cause
    First cause → Origins of change
    Formal cause → Nature of changes
    Material Cause → What is changed
    Final cause → Reasons for change

First Cause → Final Cause (Development of Reality in Time)
Final Cause → Conclusion of changes (God's Plan / Purpose)

4} True & False
    Modal—(Necessary → Possible → Impossible)
    Empirical—(Probable → Actual → Improbable)
    Metaphysical—(Un-provable → Real → Inscrutable)

ISSUES AND FRAGMENTS

5} Sinnlich—"sensible" → "Makes sense"
   Sinnlich—"sensuous" → refers to "feelings"
   Sinnlos → Unsinnig
      Sinnlos—Not based on sense data (analytic a-priori)
      Sinnlich—Based on sense data (synthetic a-posteriori)
      Unsinnig—Without Sense (illogical—"Senseless")
   Sünde—Sin → to "sunder" → separation of "sensible" from "sensuous"
      Sinnlich → sensible (moral—"proper")
      Unsinnig → senseless (a-moral—"improper")

5} "Muss man schweigen"
   Muss → "must" (Imperative) → "should" (Recommendation)
      Schweigen → "refrain from speaking" (active → admonitory)
      Schweigen → "pass over in silence" (passive → discretionary)

IX

MORE ON SILENCE

Philosophers, given their immersions in logic and analysis, are not as fond of falsehoods or fantasies as are, say, poets. So the question, in a less veridical context, could be: When confronted with a critically admired poetic work, how does one bring fact and fantasy together into a judgment that does not value falsity, but approves of beauty and expression (and insight?).

There are many kinds of silence. There are many reasons for silence. Some reasons recognize each other. Other reasons avoid the other. One silence, not hearing any other, thinks itself alone in its solitude; silence is at the end of things, beyond noise, immune to change or comparison. Another silence may retreat into the solitude that is its refuge—thereby protecting it from the noises of its own past, as well as those noises outside the purification rites that propose the virtue of total silence. But it is not easy for any particular silence to rid itself of its own noise—much less to ignore the noises of other attempts at silence. Sometimes, though, there is nothing left but to consign ones own noise (what is left that will not be shushed) to a formal school-of-silence. These are the depositories of silenced sounds which once merited making but no longer (as is said) have any further (good) reason to be made. Other silences are younger and more political—and despite still being residually noisy, seek to consign the noises of their competitors to the ex-urbs—deeming them distracting.

Despite the distances it transverses, history is not always linear—so listen carefully when the wind is still: Listen in particular for the sounds that emanate from the barrens of nonsense past. They sometimes come from sense despised—but not yet rejected.

ISSUES AND FRAGMENTS

The most profound silences surround noises not yet sounded—not thought possible—not yet thought at all. These are mostly future sounds made in worlds that, with all our pride in for-sight, we cannot imagine. No examples can be given—because this is the very point of future silence. However, some artists, composers and film-makers are good at trying—it is their solemn calling: The music of "Pierrot Lunaire" remains an existential affront to the uninitiated—an invitation to madness. It is also an invitation to you-yourself to howl—preferably at the moon. But choose your lunar periods—it's important! Closer to home: The sighs and giggling from the adjacent motel room give good reasons for self-examination—especially when you are silent. Further away: The sound of distant galaxies colliding will someday reach the earth—perhaps anticipated (abetted) by the keenness of our electronics. But what shall we do when we hear the first sounding of the spheres? I hope some genius is still around for this. Going back: No-one understood the silent sound of sorrow after death—until Grunewald painted the Isenheim Crucifixion.

In the "The Foundations of Metaphysics of Morals" (Tr. Beck), Kant writes this provocative statement: "But reason would overstep all its bounds if it undertook to explain how pure reason can be practical, which is the same problem as explaining how freedom can be possible." (Section III, P78) Here, the empirical and the normative come face to face: An action that is not caused is free—but it also, as such, is undoable. Its justification, however, is thinkable, and so provides the basis for whatever morally can be done. An action that is not caused by interest (desire, need, gain, pleasure) but whose causality is that of a categorical (universally applicable) rule is free—for it enjoins everyone, without exception, to act accordingly. This also is not possible. But why, then, is this freedom and its "condition-less-ness" not also a constraint? Kant answers: Because rationality—not physical causality—is its source—and that, in itself, is free. But "rationality" is not so much a source as an ideal—a possibility for fusing thought and action, if only our thinking were not itself embedded in the timorous yet avaricious vessels that we are. The categorical imperative cannot be completely achieved as action—and such action, could it be it essayed, would rest on individual free choice only if action were as free as its thought. Otherwise, it has no claim for realization through freedom. Motives for action, however freely thought, are always subject to rationalization—and therefore, to a layering of contingent reasons. Kant's "a-historical" status of freedom shows an important distinction between the philosophies of

MORE ON SILENCE

Kant and Hegel—who construes the "Evolution of Spirit" as being free—but as manifest in history, and not as such in individuals. But the notion of "history"—like Kant's notion of "rationality"—is also an ideal—a normative imposition on the passing of time. Kant indicates that freedom can be thought. But then, he asks how freedom (the basis for its own thinking) is itself possible—and to this he answers that there is no answer—only silence. This shows the limits of benign linguistic regress in philosophy—and a recognition (to which Wittgenstein also subscribes) that there are realms beyond analysis that can be thought but not asserted—but are essential (if only as a constraint) to what it is that can be asserted.

Kant's differentiation—between "end" and "limit"—is also important for Wittgenstein's notion of silence. It is not an end to philosophy that the latter is proposing, but a limit on what philosophy should be concerned with. Hegel's evolutionism is more ambitious—for it includes rationality within historical process. For Kant, however, a "causality of freedom" is individual. It is not a misnomer, but rather signifies a collision between realms—empirical and speculative—about what sort of content, when extracted from this apparently contradictory phrase, would be revealed. It could only be a fusion of obligation and desire, and a transgression of the limits to which each such manifestation (and manifest-being) belongs. This, to my mind, is tantamount to expanding the principles of understanding—if they are taken in the broader sense that includes reason and its reflection. Silence, then, in Kant's construal of freedom, and in Wittgenstein's admonition in the Tractatus, are both prescriptive—they indicate a limit on what can sensibly be said within a specific context of discourse. But Kant does not, and Wittgenstein comes not to, assert that limit for all discourse. The early Wittgenstein sometimes sounds as if there is only one realm (and method) worthy of discussion. He later reverses this in favor of considering language to be a multiplicity of games and rules—that one plays preferentially. Kant presents different realms and their relevant discourses early on in his works—but a good part of his philosophical struggle was against theological efforts to conflate realms (sacred and secular) through a presumption of overall adequacy through a single discourse. Kant succeeded in his struggle, much to the chagrin of religionists, who responded—as the story goes—by naming their pet dogs "Kant."

Kant believed that his categorical constructs—as they are rational, not empirical—are universal and necessary. They are, in effect, unchanging (the a-priori conditions of thinking itself) for they underlay all scientific, moral, and aesthetic thought—which, of course, does change, but remains coherent between temporal changes through the continuity of categorical distinctions. Wittgenstein's analyses of life and language are less confidant but more dynamic- more subject to revision: Situations that are as yet unthought, are as yet unspoken. When such do occur, they will require new linguistic rules for their understanding.

Wittgenstein's acknowledgment of the multiplicity of language forms is found in his later opus—the "Philosophical Investigations." (1953, Tr. Anscombe). In criticizing his own early theories, Wittgenstein states: "A picture held us captive. And we could not get outside it, for it lay in our languages and language seemed to repeat itself to us inexorably." (PI, 115) This captivity supposes a unity within its boundaries of which picturing provides a holistic representation. But the plethora of pictures and the strain imposed by the effort to keep unwelcome (illogical, nonsensical, unreadable) pictures out, leads to this statement: "in philosophy, we often compare the use of words with games and calculi that have fixed rules, but cannot say that someone who is using language *must* be playing such a game—but if you say that our languages only *approximate* to such calculi, you are standing on the very brink of a misunderstanding. For then it may look as if we what we were talking about were an *ideal* language." (PI, 81) At this point, for Wittgenstein, there is no longer the ideal of an ideal language against which all others can be compared and corrected—rather, there are "forms of life," of which the different language-games are expressions. Between these, there are "family resemblances" through which games are identified as part of the human enterprise—and through examination of the constants on which these "family" similarities are based, might rid the whole (also a Kantian hope) of misleading and debilitating beliefs. In response to criticism of these changes in his thesis, he writes: " (to those who say)—I am interested in the pure article, I want to say: we misunderstand the role of the ideal in our language. That is to say, we too should call it a game." (PI, 100) As to the thesis of "family resemblances," he writes poetically: "I can think of no better expression to characterize these similarities than "family resemblances"; for the various resemblances between members of a family: build, features, color of eyes, gait, temperament, etc. etc. overlap and crisscross in the same way. And I shall say: 'games' form a family." (PI, 67)

I turn now to the issue discussed in an earlier chapter: "Wittgenstein and Silence." How does this turn—from "language as picture" to "language as game"—affect the admonition that ends the Tractatus—"muss man

MORE ON SILENCE

schweigen?" Do language games all require the catharsis of silencing? An evident answer to this should be "no." Language games are like their users, in that they proliferate, interbreed, thrive, experience difficulties, become obsolete– only to return through renewal and renaming. Games, unlike pictures, are not aspirants subject to the single ideal of logical clarity, and the terrible swift swords of Frege, Vasari, or Saint Michael. Instead, they play according to the rules that have formed them—internally consistent, but different from the game being played next door—not to say a neighborhood, or a continent away. There is another passage which needs looking at in this regard: "The real discovery is the one that makes me capable of stopping doing philosophy when I want to—the one that gives philosophy peace, so that it no longer is tormented by questions which bring *itself* into question." (PI, 133) A philosophical farewell party with silence as the speaker! Necessity and continuity are pushed out of the heavens and fall to the pavement with a thud. The streets are full of noise and people. No silence there.

A friend comes, with a token gift, to a party I am making. The label on the package reads—"Goat Cheese." I mumble a few words of thanks and fall silent. Actually, it would have been no better had the label read—"Cow Cheese." Then, in small print on the inside label, the meaning becomes more evident: "Chevre." Oh! That cheese is now in a different language game. We are in the bucolic French countryside. I say to her: "There is a box of crackers and a spreading knife on the table near the window. I will pour the wine. Here—have a bite and take a sip. Salty and sweet! Good for talking.

X

CROOKED AND STRAIGHT

AT AN OLDER TIME and in another place, I wrote a story in which the distinctions there discussed became personalized. The story concerns a division of peoples into opposing social categories in accordance with their beliefs, body-types, sexual inclinations, professions, political concerns, eating habits, wealth, ancestry—and the like. Then, I also called it "The Crooked and The Straight." Its premise—then and now—is of a basic categorical distinction that informs our interplay with other people. Here, I have both added to and subtracted from the earlier version, and have modified its role by imposing onto it a different set of conditions—one more suited to my present purposes.

Categorizing people, it may be objected, is an immoral as well as a conceptually flawed endeavor: It can be called a form of imprisonment without cause—and is more based on fashion, prejudice, and power, than on any list of scientific criteria. Actually, I agree with this—but my discussion has other, more hypothetical, purposes.

But it should be said, beforehand, that "categorization"—whether done formally, in passing, or through the permissiveness of fiction—is one of the basic human interactions. No one is immune from being compared, placed and displaced—at any time of life. Every-one that one knows is—used to—or will be—an "F" or a "G." Such designations follow from birthing-place to school—from marriage-bed to death-bed. One is always a something or other—as found in the board-room, living-room, hospital-room, bedroom—and even in the people-less void where you would—if you could—go to avoid all this. But arriving there—finally free—you must admit that of all external comparisons given you, you best fit the categories given you by yourself. This justifies, or at least, condones the trip.

CROOKED AND STRAIGHT

So you should accept it: There is no "you-pure." You are multiple—identified and packaged through identities which are not only yours—although some may strive, with due elaboration—to make it appear so. But taken together—in both memory and prediction—the "you's" that accumulate upon the nascent you in order to make the "actual you"—becomes the story of your life. This is true of my life too. The "real you" is a different matter—one which I will take up later.

For the purposes of this story, I submit that we are all children, respectively, of the Crookeds and the Straights—although the battle that has raged between these factions shows little sign of abating. (Be patient, the distinction will out—just read along). If you are unsure as to which side you're on—select your preference during the morning pee, and compare it with the one you subscribe to after dinner. The comparison is a good way to learn who and what you are. Remember though, that categories—even at their most adamant—are like the changing landscapes of mountains and deserts, sky and water. Climate counts! They are also like high-rises and ruins. History counts! Some mirror beauty, and others decrepitude. Love counts! But also be grateful for the seductions of change. Come to appreciate the proclivity of time in dissolving old categories and creating new ones. Don't be surprised, however, if the identity you have arisen-to at morning, is not to your liking come afternoon. Love always looks different before daybreak. But if you are such a Straight as to need the safety of continuing identities—understand that they, like good wine, must be properly aged, and only tasted in the most supportive light—otherwise they change.

The prophets of progress sing that the resolution of all conflicts is just around the corner. The cosmic dialectic, however—largely indifferent to us—works instead to give time its own determinate content. But in our particular time, the prophetic chants of anticipated progress cannot long remain in "plain-song." Look and listen! Young curiosity about the future will soon fold simple opposition into the tantrums of "rap." Or, if teleology is still with us—we will be illuminated through the complexities of "neo-counterpoint" (thank you Miles and Monk)—which will take us straight up the crooked road. If that is not enough—or will not do it—then we find that "music as noise-attended-to" (by, say, Varese and Cage), will push the slower things along—although going down that road may well be hazardous: They say it ends around the bend.

I have travelled some of the lands contested by these hostile factions. They do not engage in war right now, but they still throw stones when twilight makes recognizing friend-from-foe quite difficult—and mugging innocents more easy. I was younger when I made these journeys, and was more fascinated by differences in the taste of shape, the sound of smell—and the exquisite costumes worn by predators and girlfriends. I was less interested in territory or polemical disputes than in (pardon) "forms-of-life." But even then you could find me in the mummer-show of mingling– which showed me to appreciate the subtle set of contrasts found in the borders between soft grass and rock—or soft hair and bare flesh. Such borders are the common ground of mergers—of dark and light, sweet and salty, slow and fast, soft and loud—and all the other mergers one makes or needs to make things go. Back then, however, especially on the meaner city streets, and particularly after darkening time, it was harder (unless you got real close) to determine which passer-by was straight or crooked, or some of both—and would (or would not) be waiting to do you, when you turn your back to round the corner and look for someone more or less like you.

After living eighty years or so, and despite my early swoops and swerves (I was born and nurtured simple-straight) I am now composite. From secret childhood on, I have had crooked proclivities—as is evidenced by my interest in curves, birds, and those irrational angles found outside the charts. Recently, I traveled again to those still-contentious lands where I was born—just to see how it is to live there in these now latter days. However, I must insist to the younger critics (are you still there?) that the journey was made to affirm (to me—not you) that I am no closer to where my (true) allegiances lie than I was when I first was born. Yes, I am now back, bemused at the insistence of indecision, and a little tired of making trips and taking naps. But coming back from then and there, I find changes made back right here—without permission, but all around me—changes that show me as more obsolete than I want to be. After I intone the required "alas"—I see them, those changelings—preening in the noonday sun—indulging in the most recent best of grass and flesh—and proudly labeled as the latest thing.

So, in defense, I turn to the more unruly vectors: Looking back, I see that the straightest roads are taken by those who ride in power. Looking forward, I argue (for the collective good of Crookeds) that straight roads—especially those built by Straights for when they too get old and crooked—are to be avoided. But wouldn't you know it—few of my friends will listen. They slyly say that "road" is itself a metaphor—be it primrose path, hard slog, or the more literary crooked-straight. In my friendly way, I insist—quite ecumenically—that we all have a fulsome map of roads to follow—whatever our beliefs and purposes. But such mealy-mouthing will not do: The young—those really with-it—snicker: Isn't it tacky—and boring too, they say—to describe the future with such locutions as "the road?" Talking about the future in such ways is, after-all, a mix of Hegel's Geist and Dorothy's yellow-brick-road—neither of which went anywhere: Dorothy got old and put-upon; and Geist is battling revisionists in the Eastern world—so "road," even as a metaphor, does not describe a way to the future. Everybody flies these days—and those who do not—float. Some crash and others sink. The real conundrum, however, is that you equate the future with every passing moment of your life—but you're never actually there.

I admit that I no longer fly nor float—but I will give my thesis one more shot. I ask: Don't you want to know the best way to get to a there that is the best of anywhere and everywhere? There is a where, as you should know, to which we all want to go—both actually and really. But wouldn't you know it—they don't listen—those milk sops. They just turn snickering into mutters. Conundrums, too, they say, are boring. If you're wanting and can't talk—take a bargain flight—and when the rapture comes—speak in tongues. Or, if that scares you—just stay home and watch the box.

I see now that many of my old-time buddies in the market-place, once attentive at the foot of Socrates, early scratchers at insurgence and seekers of excess—are gone: They have become straighter than even geometry provides. Most now insist—for hallowed reasons they won't reveal—that they are sworn enemies of the Crookeds. But I will take them on: My early narratives about the Crooked and the Straight provide material—people (if you want to commingle) with which to fill-in, or flesh-out, or choose between—the personae that I offer as inhabitants of the categories I present.

But- reader—you are free to introduce your own materials to these categories—even if they don't easily or consistently match my own descriptions. (I am not obsessive). You may want, e.g., to distinguish between the allure of freedom and the need for equality. In that case, I suggest that you consider the prolix possibilities of Straight and Crooked as they intersect with Mind and Spirit. (It makes for a great theme with which to rescue art). But don't be too tight about it. You can always try other ways: Indulge your loves; skewer your foes; ignore those (as you see fit) who do not live in your world; bad-mouth those (if you must) whom you despise for reasons you need not divulge; avoid the ones (if you can) who are young, bright, and will run right over you. But be free, always, to change your mind—even before, and certainly as—and after—you grow older.

XI

WALKS FOR THE TAKING

I RECENTLY CAME ACROSS a club across town (at the junction of the new super-highway and the old dirt road) that caters to a variety of ecumenical folk—who call themselves "The Crookeds." They party well! Why choose a single way, they sing, when one can do the double trouble—and play it, at once sashaying with a crooked gait, while standing (almost) straight when being (just perceivably) on-the-move. What with life so short, and worthwhile goals ensconced in mostly petty minds—but yet so far away from needy hands—why not try a cosmic combination where you will both succeed and fail—both die and be immortal. All you need is to avoid the local versions of adamant conviction. While doing all of this, it helps to swing and sway—and when you're tired, to find a fall into a waiting soft embrace.

Come—take a walk with me: Do you not see the hills without valleys and the ponds that are neither deep nor shallow? Look both ways: There, lurking in the twilight just behind the prickle bushes are the lions and tigers and bears of olden days. Don't be afraid. They, denizens of those better days, should be welcome even when they bite—for fleshly blood has (should have) a way of passing beyond its seepage of becoming, into the free-flow realm of being. That's something for all of us to consider at the times we bleed.

But when it is the snake that bites, the blood congeals—and the poison travels through to eat your marrow and still your heart. Then what will you—dying—do with your remaining time? In extremis, you could say to those who hover, that there are no good reasons for you to live as they still do. But then you must affirm with your remaining breath, that there are good reasons to live as you once did—until that snake got through to you.

WALKS FOR THE TAKING

But we always have the voices from other side: If you had been careful and suitably ambitious, say the straights, you (at all costs) would have avoided the irrationality of angry snakes—as well as slanted shadows, inchoate whisperings and titterings that solicit obscene response, proffer glimpses of a naked thigh, and unfold the futuristic joy of non-Euclidian geometry. These are all signposts of evil-in-our-time. Your slightest interest in the one or other will cause the Demons to pull you down before you reach retirement. But there are, I admit, some Demons (just a few remaining) who, for Lycanthropic reasons, like to act early—before the deed is done. They prefer the younger sinners, and will wait around to pounce on you the moment you step off the straightaway onto some beguiling patch of dewy grass—that precarious early moment when you first discover how it is to wet both feet at the same time—and let the wetness move from down the sole to between the toes, and then to where it later may or may not go. These special Demons adore first-blood—it tastes, they say, like a first pressing of the grape. Most other Demons (the majority) remain more circumspect—waiting, as their contract states, to choose the moment when you, having grown a bit, wade further into choppy waters—chanting a grown-up song, and sloshing bravely through the now deeply swaying reeds. You, in all innocence (as you will later plead) were only watching minnows, and did not notice the limbs of wantons moving in the water—until you got a leg wrapped round your neck, and were pulled down beneath the waves.

There are still other Demons (the "Demonology" has almost as many volumes as the Britannica). They are the older corporate type of Demon—those who prize "original intent" (Hell has it's own chronicles of achievement). Such Demons do not like the diabolical use of wantons: After all, as they say: "These women—even when situated in the new permissiveness—are duplicitous. They are all descendants of that female who first bit the apple before her male friend—from whose rib (you know) she came—could reach it. And then she gave him the second bite to insure his continuing service when they had to move to less imposing quarters. Her forbears—Succubi and Incubi, as they are called—have been sent down to democratize our ranks. But—as we all know—they have become too independent and competitive. These women—I must tell you—they want it all—and these days are following their own agenda. Yes—they still torment their victims—that's their role in the big picture—but they do it in those hidden ways that fit contemporary tastes."

ISSUES AND FRAGMENTS

But do not fear, you unrepentant sinners—whatever are your tastes and preferences—that you will be excluded from the dooms-day schedule of performances. You have a ticket. And remember: You have, through the years, been designated as players—and we, the demons, wantons, imps, and sundry sadists—want to play our parts—with you. We will gleefully perform (with you) in that ever-changing array of demonic scenarios (those foul interjections of gross depravity—pain, pleasure, and in-between) that deny everything you once believed in. Being caught in the "Big Lie" guarantees you full entrance into the unending attractions of Hell. We will give you a choice (irrevocable of course) of what is the better of the worst. That done, you will be forced (against your will) to be cast into that awful place of legend where you (as you must) will play your assigned part in the obscene scenarios of demonic fantasy that you've dreamt (but not told anyone) about. Oh-yes! I know that you know the ones!

These scenarios all stem from the unsolved paradox about the first copulation that occurred before—or was it after—the expulsion. You remember going down the dusty path with only vermin and dry weeds for food—and learning how to shit in the sand beside the road. Do you also remember performing in the later plays? As the archives tell it: You embraced the role (the one the Devil taught you) of make-believe (He lied so well abut the apple's innocence)—that you thought existence would be fun. The role you later played (when you were on your own) showed your life on earth to be one of pain and violation—inflicted (incredibly) by the very ones you first birthed and weaned—those who, by any rational measure, should have strictly been all-loving to everything that comprises you. But they had free will and evidently found other measures with which to decide about you. I must say this, however: God made a mistake in fashioning a second one from the first one's rib. They should each have started together with an equal number—equally given—at the same beginning. There might then have been fewer wars.

Such corrupt visions (the straights will thunder)—whether they come from sultry southern shores, or during pensive morning ablutions, or within your sweaty nighttime bed—all these have pernicious consequences. Realize that they are conjured by playwrights of the Infernal Theatre—designed for scripts that are calculated to define your essence just when it becomes captive to your appetites. But if you do not relish aspic-of-essence as an only meal, the Chefs-from-Hell will bake a cassoulet so plump and fully fashioned (don't ask what's in it) that, when finally you are stuffed, you will be content to rest and ruminate—not thinking or praying—just farting along with friends you've made along the dusty road. But after the last gas has passed, the friends are gone, and all the leaves have fallen—you will be alone again, emptier than before, in the palest moonlight that shows only a coruscation of dead leaves. Then you too—will go.

Oh dear! I hate it (don't you?) when Straights tell those stories. What do they know? So, with my winey breath, I answer back to confront those unbearable tight-ass-holes and their sweaty morality-tales. Look to yourselves, I say. You are putting my rites of passage into your own story—and twisting it for your purposes. This is actionable—I have good lawyers—don't provoke me. And notice further: You did not omit a single part I wrote that covertly titillates you—you watched my stolen tapes with your smarmy friends. But you roared in public that such permissiveness—approaching mortal sin—confirms the negative aspects of the crooked agenda. You did this with such punitive glee—not omitting any inflammatory word—or any scenario of deviance that you remember—nor any innuendo about hidden disclosures in reserve for later trials. In response, I will offer you—for free—the fate that you assign to me.

Just think of what you will face (when you are in Hell instead of me): Brimstone and fried toads with rancid vinegar for supper; days of obligatory viewings of really dirty pictures; and the horror of well-done wantons clutching at your shrunken entrails throughout the steamy nights. (The nights in Hell, as you will come to know, are long and hot).

Then having so situated you, I will (yes) I will redeem you. I must sacrifice my pleasures (as my God commands) for all our goodness sake—and so I take onto myself what you think is rightly yours—but I also give you what you covet that is mine. I will, in company with you, embrace the joys of truth and beauty. I will forsake old wantons and the best of recent porn. I will stop eating even high-class toads—whatever are their origins. Instead, I will patiently suffer the scanty and odorless clouds of abstemious salvation, so that I can hover—float near and yet so far above the burning, fuming, and eternally hopping flesh—that (undeserved as sinners all insist) is the way one is in Hell. Yet, even in that cauldron, you will not be far from me (instant cosmic view having been perfected) not so far that I can't see and hear the sequential moments—however long drawn out—of your eventual conversion to the lower pleasures that the Devil has deemed proper for your stay in Hell. Yes! Yes! I assure you. You will come to like all that.

But, straight-o-mine, if my ending doesn't move you—then pull yourself up, cast aside the imagery that (confess!) you were beginning to appreciate, and try again to contemplate the salutary resilience of a pared-down, four-square, good and evil—not so much as exhibited by you or me, of course—but in the images (easy to find these days) that show the underlying nature of all that there is—beyond the seeming that we, the walking wounded—licentious or portentous—still live by.

I offer you an example: There is the notion—as evidenced in the programs of the older Crookeds—that a straight line is the mark of the Devil. As confirmation, they tell us to consider the following: The posture of a striking snake is a straight-line—moving, to be sure—but fully extended just before it bites. But after the bite (the offering of the apple) its purpose having been achieved—it changes. Then, both snake and line revert to the crooked-coil (the Devil's original mark) that the snake had before you stumbled and disturbed its search for little furry things—so that it had to bite you instead. That was your mistake.

A mistake for the snake—my shuddering Straight in response will cry. The snake has spent its venom and not got food—and I (through no fault of mine) am getting dead. A straight line, then—in this panoply of errors- is a failed assault, a mere happenstance—dangerous for particulars—but not harmful to the greater category of things that matter. Crookeds of all persuasions eventually straighten out and try, as best they can, to avoid the bite. That's what "path" is all about.

An academic who is Crooked, a friend of mine (yes, there are still some ensconced in ivy) might counter in this way: I must say that straightness is a shallow way to address a complex question: To ask, e.g., "what is the meaning of life?" should be answered by how well (fully) we now live and love—and that in turn, entails the divergent—variously slanted options (from all those hovering around) that enables us to select the way we want to live. Snakes cannot do this—they just bite, lay eggs, and produce other snakes that bite. For them, it's just Heaven or Hell—the straight line or the coil. But you who could have (straight friend of mine) but still don't want to—live crookedly—even in the fragrant season—will not agree.

But there always is a compromise: Think about the "spiral." This is a form that always takes you somewhere—but never too quickly or directly. Indeed, while spiraling you feel in charge—still able to reach for the golden rings that hang on branches all along the way. You'll catch some—though not all. And if you rub them (carefully, now)—they will give you the configurations that summon you to pray, or show you how best to play.

Imagine the spokes of a bent wheel that is still moving and turning. Its direction is erratic, determined by occasional tilting off the vertical of the straight and narrow into unpredictably crooked diagonals. A flawed wheel—a hand-made sin, the Straights will call it—caused by venality, chance, poor design, or the inscrutability of God's will. The Crookeds disagree: Don't you see? God's motives are transparent! He needs flaws through which to encourage the Devil to leave his lair from time to time, and so keep the cosmos moving in interesting ways. Straights invariably leave out too many of life's tilts and swerves—and instead, try to convince the undecided that the achievement of not falling—by assiduously avoiding the heat of glens and the curves of valleys—will make the straight-path free from temptation. But Crookeds, as they are more attuned to the transience of mortality, do not accept this version of the travelled time-of-life. They are not about to put off earthly pleasure for the happiness of dullness-after-death. Crookeds are more focused on the now. In what other time, they ask—can pleasure so directly be experienced? But Straights—like sophomores—are programmed to not listen. They will continue to maintain that the smell of Heavenly Bliss—unlike that grubby, earthly, body-odor—is the end worth waiting for.

Such a dispute can be confusing to both sides: Consider the recent Sunday sermons by our new minister who says he tries to demonstrate (with fulsome anecdote) the practices of evil—so as to fix them as negatives in our minds. He is much taken—as he admitted at a Friday communal dinner—by the spectacle of Bosch's sinners rent and rendered by fearsome lizards. (He also likes to consider, in detail, the torments of Saint Agatha). But some parishioners have objected. They say his hidden purpose is pornographic, and that representations of evil can themselves be evil, for they cast a too-revealing light on what should remain forever hidden—out of mind and away from the frailties of body, and the consequent vulnerability of soul.

Even some of my older crooked friends agree that pleasure is not entirely self-justifying. In the evenings, they reminisce by bringing out their old collections—tattered magazines and fragile film-strips that display the sounds and pictures, the lamentations and gestures that are the arcane language of old evil. My friends will ruefully express their dismay while continuing to watch. They do not denigrate the simple technology—nor do they criticize the now-dead flaccid bodies. Theirs is a higher criticism: These relics of a simpler, yet more predatory past—however artfully concealed—bring us nothing but a later awareness of that most pernicious evil—the translation of pain and shame into pleasure or money. Do you think, they ask indignantly, that those beleaguered folks (the actors, not the characters portrayed) did such things for pleasure—rather than money?

>   Away together—we will cry.
>   As the clear crow disdains the dark night
>   and flies innocent into the early sun—
> so must you and I avoid the pricks and pleadings
>   of both satanic and pietistic pornography.
>   With us, as we fly, we take only those who fit
>   the glad-bag of enlightened affirmation—
>   anticipating—it should be evident,
>   their bright-eyed admiration.

But such distinctions and distractions do not always satisfy the peace process. Someday, cry the straightest Straights, evil will assuredly return. And confronting it—as you can see beneath the rictus of my soon dead but once most deadly face—are only graven images of the still-powerful soldiers of consistency, abstemiousness, and righteous anger.

We should show more contempt for our enemies. We should cry: Deny them, and dismember them! I, for one, will get to the blessed footprint that is there. I will go straight through to the central gate of Heaven—unlike those crooked-snookered souls who say they also journey there—but hit every cheap motel en route. Our way, in contrast—however calumniated by the opposition as too narrow—is, I assure you, on the right side (the missionary position) of the ancient map that shows the road to eternal bliss.

So, dear my kiddies, don't listen to the dirty stories of that misbegotten preacher. (I suspect that he's a Crooked plant). You must instead be clear about the way you want to go. It's getting to be your time now—you are older—it's around that time to proceed to the starting gate of the beginning of the end. What with your shiny faces and firm impassioned tread—you can do it, yes you can.

But what is it I hear? The sounds of ambivalence are getting closer. Pleadings and complaining, grumblings and whining! After all my teaching and entreating, am I to understand that you are not quite ready yet? Speak louder and come here into the brighter light of day! Yes, oh yes, alas, I can see the quivering of too-early fattened cheeks, the blinking bloodshot eyes, the flaccid pudgy limbs—none of which bode well for a commitment to direct ascent. Too bad. So sad. You may have to—some of you—go further down and round-about to find the way.

But—oh well—I also (I must) say to you: You are allowed (these days) to be skeptical of prescribed true-belief. It's now a personal decision—not like in the old days. But it's also something more: Neither the world nor I (and I say this in strict confidence) really knows the right direction of the Straight-of-Ways. Too firm belief on this score has been the very devil for our given mandate. There are so many factions now—and they make a muddle of our attempts to pin down the self-evident path of righteousness. Times, alas, do change—although the subject of true belief, of course, does not.

Yet, I fear that confusion about specifics can lead to continued controversy. So I further say to you: Rather than having you succumb to the greater evil of total non-belief (often caused by the excessive rigors of true-belief) I give you an out: If you can't, just can't, really cannot—stand it here, there is a different path to take—which, in its eccentric curvy way, still claims the same rights of original and final goal as we do. The proponents of this path call themselves the Crookeds—in contrast, as you have undoubtedly heard, to our calling ourselves—the Straights.

Because the distinction is more a matter of practice than doctrine, you can spot a Crooked easily. They are less steadfast in bearing than we (they being mostly fat, often short, and easily winded—although the young ones can be quite beautiful). Also—they tend to eat and drink too much. They are accommodating in theory but duplicitous in practice—and there is not a firm categorical distinction anywhere in their bones.

In fairness, however, I must admit that, despite their flat feet, and the sweet-and-sour smell that hovers over their ambivalence about most everything, they still are bona-fide members of our universal club which, for various ideological, historical, and prudental reasons, has recently (at a meeting in Austin) named itself: The Congregation of Straights and Crookeds."

When pressed, the faction to which I belong, describes the term 'Straight' as indicating directness, clarity, abstemiousness. Their long-term aim in life is to appropriate (as is due them) the best seats in Heaven. The other faction, which calls itself the "Crooked," say that their name connotes multi-directionality rather than deformity: A Crooked is not warped but flexible—this by dint of constant bending and swaying—a good approach to the enjoyment of right-here life. Crookeds do not see themselves as irretrievably—or even slightly—deviant (although this is sometimes insinuated by the most pointy-nosed of Straights). Rather, Crookeds see them-selves as sensible.

The more ecumenical Straights now react (with some guilt) to accusations concerning their previous intolerance. They now accept that Crookeds (poor benighted souls, they say) can seek a middle ground between doctrinal inflexibility and directionless relativism. They also agree (uneasily) that Crookeds should be counted as members of the loyal opposition. This rational has historical roots: We should all remember what continues to happen: When war with the Shapeless-Formless (those mindless spawns of antiquarian beliefs and despoilers in the sand of distant lands) seemed inevitable—the crookeds did join with us: They prepared food, rolled bandages, and contributed to the cadences of the Long March. (But we straights, it must be said, did most of the fighting).

Back to now: If you are still interested, my dears, in the more comfortable route to true belief, you can find the dwelling place of Crookeds by crossing the street directly in front of the old-home church, and then bearing one block left. Those crooked folks (incredibly) have built a new and shiny temple, whose outer courtyard includes a coffee shop that serves robust European blends and (sinfully) exotic pastries. If you go further back inside, sweet-smelling odors celebrate a barbeque-emporium that, the natives insist, provides the best ribs to be found this side of non-belief.

Although my advice to you is to merely try them out—I must tell you—even that has generated trouble for me at the temple. Listen to the comments of my peers: "Balderdash, poppycock, blasphemy and bullshit" is the cry—even from my dearest friends among the Straights. These crooked leftist rascals, they say to me—to which you would so blithely send our children—will soft-sell their hedonistic ways and promote a no-sweat path to get to where we—through our efforts to make the Straight more narrow, and the Crooked straighter—refuse to walk. We—not they—are headed to the source of true belief—and the indifference of our children to our efforts will be your fault.

But after this—although bloodied—I must disagree with my friends. A needed reformulation of ancient verities always brings criticism—particularly from the old folks of worn belief. But there is hope for renewal: Just look up the road, I tell the young ones. There are no Straight-and-Narrows to be seen out in the suburbs—except for those living near the trailhead that borders the stagnant bog that has the old-time smell. If you are interested in sadness, it's worth a trip to talk with those forlorn creatures. But after days of dry and musty natter, you will ask yourselves why anyone would choose to live with the mosquitoes and mire of narrow choice—and forsake the consolations of barbeque, beer, and poetry?

Crookeds offer alternatives (such being their stock-in-trade) that try to show they are both believers and up-to-date. The food at the Krooked-Klub Motel is quite good—although a bit greasy—and the portions are for my tastes too large. The rooms are well furnished in a tacky sort of way, and the TV offers pay-erotica. When you leave (the check-out time is a considerate 1 pm) the recommended exit takes you down a smooth path leading to a well-paved road that eventually merges (yes it does) with a cross-country super-highway—that goes, of course, to everywhere.

Now let's pull back a bit. I must, for fairness' sake, confess that I have over-vilified the opposition—even though, nominally, they are still (with) us. Actually—I must (quietly) say to you—it doesn't really matter which road you take. All roads will eventually get you to where you want to go. But be careful. Take note of the friction factor in your decisions on both belief and travel. The Narrow-Straights seek out roads that go interminably up-hill, and they often are undermined by the painful rubbings of bunions and the parching effect of dry penance in thin air. The better-lubricated Crookeds do not do pain well—they will sit around and cry for help before it hurts. Even in the wilderness, they prefer amenities—ski lifts, chalets, foot-massages and the like—to dogged slogging up or falling down—steep hills.

But in the long run, all roads cross. Caravans that came from opposite directions in the early times, found companionship in places like the Dalles—where only traders in skins and whisky used to meet. Some of them prayed and sometimes wondered why they came—and so it was that bands of Straights and Crookeds could reach the juncture where unbelievers would not venture. They first came for mutual protection, and then to sit and eat together. Of course, much else followed. Some still attribute such meetings to coincidence—but if shown the old photographs, they will reminisce about their sharing of traded goods and strong whiskey, and their coming together in warming beds.

For are we not, we and they—(the wiser ones on both sides will say)—are we not all really of the same persuasion? Not quite—not yet—but it could be so with some more work.

Sadly, the wanted union has not yet come. It's the continued grindings of an old-old story: The Straights are Dualists. For them, there is a never-ending war between good and evil. They hold that evil, even in disguise, has no access to true belief: Smell the stench, they say—sickly-sweet at times, rancid-sour at others—that identifies the source of evil which—despite the new detergents and old perfumes—has remained pervasive throughout eternity. (It will creep along the pews, and slither over convent walls—it twists connubial beds with off-center urgings—and it will bring hot sweat to the groins of innocents). Note this—the narrowest of the Straights insist: Evil is the other to everything that should be. Evil fills its still-eternal time by undermining the out-lying shoulders of the narrow way—so as to make it rife for the faithful's falling.

Evil was once considered absolute by Straights of every persuasion. But when looked at now—within the wider swings and echoes of recent times—some straights believe that evil can (in good faith) be shunted into the more malleable context of the barely tolerable. Once there, freed from the onus of the Diabolical, evil can be further nudged to where what once was sinful is now permitted into the outermost rings of the merely unacceptable—the outer-most suburbs of the Good.

The Crookeds, in contrast, while they do not deny the presence of evil, do not regard it as absolutely other. Crookeds are not Dualists—but Monists. For them, all oppositions eventually reconcile and become one. The spiral is their alternative to both the circle and the straight and narrow—for unlike its single-lined competitors, the spiral has expanding and contracting latitude to envelop different interests within its swirl. It is also less direct—less brutal—more accommodating—even more gracious—a shape to party with.

All this change comes slowly, mind you, as in the digestion of a big snake's catch. The old evil cannot fulfill the needs of a new world-view—except by diminishing its contrast with the Good. In this transformation, both good and evil divide into positions of varying schools of beneficence and malfeasance: Necessary evil then becomes contingent—in keeping with the increasing worldliness of the once transcendent good—as they both now open, first to prudence, then to the practicality of their callings.

According to the grand plan of the Crookeds—when evil is brought into the subtleties of discourse about right and wrong and in-between—and its proponents are exposed to facials, pedicures, and a soothing massage—it (evil) will—never completely but increasingly—shed the scaly skin of dependence on its Satanic source. Crookeds want to transform evil into an energizing variant—a gadfly of the now stationary Good. This encourages evil, however unwittingly, to become a participant in the next stage of a better—more efficient, more conversant—Good.

XII

THE GOOD

But goodness knows where the Good resides.

Kant hypothesizes that it is only to be found in a good will—as documented through a self-examining measure that provides, but cannot mandate, a universal guide for the rule-governed particulars of moral action.

That measure, however, is only an ideal—one that, in bad times seems counter-intuitive—an ideal that no one can (or would want to) live up to. But these contraries—between autonomy and contingency—as he notes, are for the will to resolve in practice: Morality is a task—leading, if rationally willed (within a supportive disposition) to the good.

Schopenhauer, more pessimistically, holds that will is categorically destructive, and yet all-pervasive, but must in any case be overcome (also an ideal)—in order for the individual to achieve a selfless goodness—a recognition of the "Idea," which is modeled on participation in the (Platonic) Form of Good. But this is easier done in a context of withdrawal than it is in one of engagement. The inclinations supported by the will are too strong to be challenged—they must be side stepped. If you are so inclined, says Schopenhauer, listen to music (he particularly liked Rossini). When listening to music, you will find all you need of happiness and despair, joy and sorrow, resolution and dissonance—and it's all there without the pain. In music, the will is transformed by its representations into the sublimated experience of rationality, peace, and pleasure—whatever are its manifestations in actual living.

Hegel thinks that the Good comes out best in the end—where it corresponds to the final stage of Spirit. But the way to this ideal is indifferent to the contingent fortunes of the wayfarer. Neither quick nor dead—nor vegetable or mineral—monarch nor subject—seem to have much to do with

THE GOOD

historical necessity—the inevitability—of this final achievement. What, indeed, could reverse the "Evolution of Spirit?" Hegel did not fear the Devil—he had the flux of history as support. Indeed, there are the Hegelian "world-historical-individuals" whose exploits move the process along. But their individual fates (c.f. Napoleon, or Caesar) do not counter the eventuality of later achievement. But they provide good reading. Scattered along the historical way are the dramatic (often theatrical) accounts of contenders for historical immortality. For the rest of humanity, however, "Spirit's Evolution" comes at a different cost. Embedded in history's development—there is the impersonal imperative of "dematerialization." This notion identifies those peoples, actions, and theories which (in Hegel's view) are largely irrelevant to the main thrusts of historical development—the "Evolution of Spirit." Hegel's criteria are largely autocratic, for they are based on, e.g., success in war, consolidation of power, territorial expansion, the development of high culture and the achievement of great art—in which successes are glorified. The discards in this narrative suffer a "historically irrelevant" materiality—an "anonymity"—that not only explains their historical failures, but also rationalizes the individual sufferings involved. For Hegel, history is neither fair nor just—it shows no pity but it's course is inevitable. This thesis of inevitability is often called "progress"—an inherent, although abstract, developmental value which can be found in Modernist theory. It also supports a materialist view that finds a way of affirming "progress" while denying "God." But its workings (as Hegel describes—Marx proposes—and Lenin articulates) can make omelets of individual lives.

For uncommitted travelers (and philoso-phobes) the road to follow that gets you to a greater goodness presents a different conundrum. Mapping the lower journey, one finds the dark trails in the forest overrun with demons that are not of your choosing—cavorting freely in the bushes. Following this lower way can also lead to enervating wallows, full of back biting gnats and suffocating sophistry.

But the way of moderation—fleeing back up the hill—is also difficult. Going high exposes one to brambles and unrelenting exposure to sun and rain—not to mention unsettling glimpses of aging showgirls who live in trailers perched on patches of barren land. Some of these saggy beauties can still give a good semblance of kicking up a heel or two—but they will not leave the sunlight (even for you) because they prefer its warmth to the cold and damp of aging crotches. After all that they've been through, they say, overheating is no problem—and they like the smell of one-time yesterdays—when these memories are no longer fresh, and molder slowly in the sun.

Yet, all these are ways of arriving at a destination—that most comprehensive place at the end of the dream of "getting-there." But where is there? Certainly not anywhere! So why choose that there? How, pilgrim, do you anyhow know about such places? You haven't been—although you won't admit it—everywhere. (I'm being too harsh). Calm down, old-timer! Don't be so upset! I'm not after your money or your wife! We should sit down, have a drink, and all agree—for we all have to play this game—that there is an acceptable there for those who need a somewhere—and that does mean all of us. Let me tell you the good news! It so happens, in this year-of-the-game, that after all the centuries of across-aisle scowling, and betting against the inevitable—the Straights and the Crookeds have come to agree that they share the objective of going somewhere—the Place of Good—the Form of Beauty—the Face of Truth. God Almighty is there too! Further, they agree that (in principle) some-such where is where we—all of us—really want to be.

But reality is a problem: Going is usually going somewhere—one-or-another way. The going that the Straights propose is a long hard way, and as one grows older, the legs tend to soften and give-in to their gimpy knees. As you know, the requisite tone for climbing requires an admixture of crookedness, straightitude, preening, good food, and a lot of working out.

Actually, we all—whatever shape we're in—may take some comfort: There are—as with martinis—many styles of mixing, established by historical debates over social purposes and proper ingredients. A martini, evidently, is not simply gin and ice—there must be the civilizing presence of fine vermouth (just a few drops, please) and a salutary consideration of garnishes—olive, lemon twist, pearl onions. All this is to encourage our having more than one.

There have been many clashes—some ancient, others recent—between our factions. But do you not remember the times when skinny, scarred and smelly Straights would wander through the outside dark—sniffing at the chic and fragrant effluence that marks the well-fed limbs of their crooked adversaries?

Then there were the nights that others might remember—when the coiffed and softly rounded Crookeds—normally reliant on an all-volunteer army—but suffering from their pent-up need for penetration without words, turned on the front-hall lights—at which time the spare and bony, attracted like moths to the zapper, forsook both envy and vituperation, and mutely acquiesced to the procedures and pleasures of a multi-hand massage.

At history's end, all such frolics are forgiven. When the journey's over, each side, without penalty, inhales the vapors that have drifted up together with the noises of the mingling. The young and curious who were conceived along the way, might however find the smells too loud. They would then want to re-invent the ancient fragrances and arrive at a new scent that would greet them—the young ones—with a freshness that befits their new ways—if they still think to come together.

The most potent scent, through centuries of planning, is based on the admixture of new prurience and old penitence. It also exemplifies the irresistible waft and taste of communal barbeque. Oh, how those tips and slabs, first dry-rubbed and then well-mopped, can smell after hours of slow smoking—like the most celestial of ambrosias. What we offer now—both factions have been heard to say—is worthy of a late-day contribution to the saga of loaves and fishes—our celebration of ecumenicity.

In keeping with those rites that have meaning in our time, we begin our celebration by stretching the plumpest of the Crookeds, brushed lightly with a red-wine and tomato marinade (made civil by a bit of oregano and some garlic) onto the rack of penitence. Heavy groans and sub-rosa pleadings can then be heard—asking to not over-do them before they're ready to be taken off. Then we throw on the rinsed-off Straights, slathered with honey, cumin and hot pepper. On the brink of browning, they are brought together with the chubbies into a comprehensive menage of fragrant flesh and willing bone. Deep squeals and diminishing denials; serial stroking in negotiation with a crisping shyness—an oratorio in the making! The caterwauls that sound till early morning are conditioned by the contrapuntal logic that reveals the inadequacies of separate voices—which voices, if left alone to sing their selfish songs, would only satisfy a solitary other—but could never project the value of an all-together—whose harmonies deny the sounds of willful separation.

If you are still concerned with missing-out—because you were a late arrival to the chorus—consider that the standpoint of eternity is not always critical of a misdirected enterprise. (You'll get yours). Failure in a cause is usually due to overreaching, but the debris of failure need not be discarded—it can be sorted out for valuable artifacts. The shards of great failures are, after all, testimonials of intense trying. Eternity (unlike modernity) is quite benevolent—even though ecumenicity is a political not a formal art, and does not flourish without some gestures towards (acceptable) progress. So be bold yet circumspect! You must find your way in all of this.

Let's get back to basics: Slow-smoked barbeque assiduously basted, is where we all come together at road's end. All conflicts about the Greater Good, whether they start in the head or gut, and however much they are separately meant to reveal another's lesser longings (or talents) are, when pressed, like pomegranates giving forth their seeds—too many to count and no good way to eat them all.

So the philosophical attempt to create certainty continues without fail, to fail. What would adjudicating between the appetites and beliefs of Straights and Crookeds come to? Is it the dry rub, the slow smoker, the careful aging, or the winy marinade that gives the best taste when the rib is offered for their eating? Does our patience sometimes falter in mid-cooking—and we reach impatiently for the secondary sausage, the sides of coleslaw and potato salad, and, yes, that ubiquitous ear of overcooked corn? Should we not have waited and had a drink or two? Wait, say's the Queen-of-Ribs, for the setting sun—she knows the best time for eating barbeque. The approach of night provides good acoustics for the sounds of chomping—and tomorrow is time enough to discard the bones.

After all these years of separation, and after having glimpsed the landscape at the joining of the roads, no one needs reverting to the path of early discord. So let us—our elders (on both sides) say—let us declare an ideological holiday. They—the elders—being old and optimistic, think that this is a really good move. Also, being old, they have fewer consequences to face if they are wrong. So they instruct us cheerfully: We should begin the festivities at both the far-left and far-right of our once acrimonious bazaar—as these have traditionally been the places that generate discord. We can contemplate the past, weigh the conflicting demands for atonement—and then, without committing ourselves, we can amble (carefully but optimistically) towards the middle.

Now—as we have reached out to one-another—we will assuredly walk together, hand–in–hand (if that doesn't bother you) along the ways that promise universal satisfaction. From these universals, small paths branch off, each dotted by grottos showing pumped-up beauties in six-inch heels, tempting you to buy what you want but do not need. Yes, a bit tasteless—this sort of greeting—but business, as we all know, is good for both sides.

THE GOOD

If you still have the will, however, to avoid taking-on too much of what you cannot finish—there are the other ways to enjoy your self. Turn right and take the path that leads uphill. You will soon hear a drone of chants inveighing against flesh—cooked or raw—whether eaten for sustenance or pleasure. The women chanting all wear flowered skirts and rope-sandals, and distribute free handouts of veggie recipes which include cautionary tales, particularly directed to the old folks, about how to avoid calories and their associated sins. The men smile, smoke cheap cigars and passable pot, and occasionally play on large guitars.

If all this makes you uncomfortable, pilgrim—if you don't like smoking—continue walking, but to the left this time. There, you will find the paths that lead to a different cuisine: In a large hut made of rattan and straw, women smelling of new perspiration offer trays of falafel and egg-rolls that cohabit shamelessly with offerings of jerked goat, fried ants, and smoked eel. The men are hairy, unwashed, laugh a lot and blow on pipes—and will occasionally beat fat large gourds with long thin sticks—when they want to hear more sound and have the world move a little faster. In the center, there is a café that serves couscous, garlic-soup, green-beans and lamb-shanks—and, from 6 to 10 pm, lightly tattooed belly dancers. When you've eaten everything you can, you can rest or go back down the hill.

There, hidden somewhat by leafy brush and pungent smoke, is an area frequented by one-time flower-children now mostly in their sixties. There also are a few remaining veterans (older still) of the wilder times of civil disobedience. When these warriors speak at all, they speak in parables—but they rarely smile. Some younger-ones speak a lot, for they had become professors before they fell—and the habit remains. But don't expect a deeper wisdom. Dropping-out was dumb—even when it was lots of fun. Lying around in the noon-day sun suits the long and tapered limbs of youth—and the early chatter was mellifluous—even as it came from mouths warped by words that were loved too much. And they didn't save the world—these lovelies—as they said they would. They only managed to set it in a nest of indolence and beauty—surrounded by clouds of silly smoke.

But beware, pilgrim—however impatient you may be with smoke and babbling—beware. The real-bad has different ways. If you think to veer further to the right—be very careful! You will find well-tended roads, an occasional gardener or guard—but few sounds and no pedestrians. These roads have hidden cameras in their trees and sullen mastiffs lurking in the driveways. They lead to nowhere that you and I—nor anyone we know and love—would want to go.

The too-pruned ways are the scary ways—they are far removed from the trails of pilgrim-feet. Those pristine ways are strategic pathways for both the privileged left and the angry right. It may be that the maintenance given to such roads signals an end to our idea of good direction. For why should anyone take a road that goes to nowhere—but circles round and round a place where no one should be—much less want to go? Going somewhere is always better—unless you prefer to just stay put and think about it. This is an option I'm now considering. But just going without a where in mind, may be evidence of a sickness of the soul. It could then be that going nowhere might (just might) be better than looking for the no-obligation-road that you and yours—all horny and uncouth—talked about when you first had begun to talk.

To switch to another wave-length: Reason's imperative these days is so in love with destination that it generates few wondrous other findings—as it once did through the notion of "Destiny riding bare-back on the Eternal Form of Being." Now, no longer satisfied with atavisms of a turgid origin, we search for the secret portal that leads to the finely honed condition of "not having been." Times have changed. "Being" is now of little account unless it distinguishes "non-being" from "never-having-been"—and then conjoins "once-having been," with the being attendant on "becoming." Such style-enhanced maneuvers—monuments of popular wonder—have these days become matters of conceptual urgency: very like, it is said, matters of accounting for fame and the bottom-line. These conceits—popular as they are—reveal the conceptual poverty that would ignore far more critical distinctions—such as those between "actuality" and "reality." These are distinctions I have, in passing, raised in earlier sections of this work. I return to them now, as they are important for my later discussions:

The first—(Actuality)—stands for concrete life—the physical world that is knowable through the laws and workings of empirical science: it also stands for the concrete entity, subject to the same laws, that we know as our physical selves. The other—(Reality)—is the category that includes actuality—and everything else that comprises us: This includes the footprints we leave, anecdotes of accomplishment and failure, secrets and scandals, love and hate—all that of us that transcends our actual lives, but is captured in dreams, memory, anecdote and fable, gossip and slander, obscurity and renewal. These extensions of our lives are always subject to being unnoticed

THE GOOD

or forgotten. For, in truth, our actual livings seldom generate a roaring—most past through with little noise. But our lives, when taken as reality, extend beyond our span of living—and what they come to none can tell. Specifically: The reality of a life is an extension of its actuality beyond the experience of those who live it.

These extensions (when you think about them) are not bewildering, nor entertaining—nor can they, after death, be calls to action. They are, however, a cause for present wonder. Once, "wonder" needed "progress" to mollify bewilderment and despair. It was comforting to know that we (or ours) are going somewhere—hopefully somewhere better. But "progress" has not survived the—still-raging—wars unblemished. In these latter days, progress has been co-opted to become the incessant drumbeat of uncontrolled commerce—practices that strive to become independent of the very people for whom the idea was invented. Wonder is now separating (painfully, by most accounts) from progress. (What, given the hegemony of market price, is there left to wonder about?) Well, we can always revert to nostalgia! I remember when wonder—like a single-malt scotch—went down with spirit and roar. The recent emergence of complex cocktails now provides ample (well programmed) nostalgia but only little bite. (I myself prefer cheap wine and heavy talk—let the others do the biting). But now that wonder and progress have accepted the safety of a legal separation (they see each other on holidays) I fear that, with each so pacified, they are susceptible to despoliation by separatists who wait for solitary souls entrapped in self-made boundaries.

But wonder, in social life, should not—even when it leads to dead-end (or deadly) places—be programmatically diluted by nostalgia: Better to suffer privation and polemical assault—war, even—than to watch spoon-fed replays of tired memory. Progress in its turn, should return to what it once was—the many-faceted story of anticipated life—a story that frightens by accounting for time-past without brag or blushing—and then dares to look at time-future through the kaleidoscope of its returning one-time lover—wonder. This is good reason for hope and Dionysian laughter.

XIII

PASSAGES

AGAIN, AND NOW AT ages reaching after eighty, I am on and off the grape. I periodically tell myself that I must stop. But why say "must," old scold? I thought you would be seen as equally divided when came time for the straight and narrow to drop off like outworn dandruff and then reveal the blossoms along-side your curvy road of non-coherence. I then remind myself that there are objections from some others: This, your road—as she hastens to tell me when the glasses have stopped clinking—is the road that has, in other climes and places, descended from the high pass of histrionic babble, down the cliffs of decreasing cogency, into the cave of snores and stupefaction.

Of course, she's right. The gadflies that once pushed me down this road remain alive—but now only in my memories. Still, they need to be shorn of their disguises (Why "shorn," old prude—I thought you have a thing for body-hair?) and stripped of the glitter that hides their squat behinds and big-foot origins. (These last remarks are more to the point, my venerable other—I, too, dislike country dancing). But on that arcane subject—stripping—tell me: Do you—as I still do—enjoy the slow undressing—the fumbling, funky emanations and suppressed giggle—the snip-snap of hooks—the slip slap and slurp when unpeeling damp corsets—the squeak and swear of untangling lacing—and the squeal of pinched and bubbling flesh—all of which begin after conversation ends and the night shows up? I admit, ol' buddy, I do—although other, more impatient, friends would say: Mere handicraft—busy-work—a waste of time and wine—bad for your blood pressure and your fingernails. But I confess to (only) you about the way it (really) was: I remember the slime I didn't wallow in, but came to read about while under my bed-covers when just a boy—when I thought, as children do, that it should be mine in which to wallow—if I so desired. My reading of the proper actions was not exactly true to later life—but close enough. I still think that such things—lordy lord—are due me. To be sure, I see procedures differently now—the mingling of breaths, when essayed late-in-life, needs careful monitoring—especially as I prefer Chardonnay to her bourbon and branch. And look you—the interstices of fruitful contact must constantly be reviewed to ascertain that none—neither a tittle nor a jot—is passed over—just because ambition wanes. But there are limits—yes there are. Come morning, and I look barefaced at the unadorned, I see again why happiness appears most clearly through a wine-dark glass. Without a drink or two, the world lacks color, focus, extravagance, magnitude, and the sweetness of unmet promise.

"Hallo Inside!" A voice from outside (it's those people, again) is heard: "A question for you: Is it not the task of an adequate representation to be accomplished within the parameters of sanity and sobriety—thereby giving the world its proper due?" I was expecting this—so I respond:

> "Tasking" is for accomplishers and overseers—
> those who believe in what you call a "due."
> It has no place, don't you know, in fucking, life, or art.
> And "proper" is for pedants—just to name a few.

My retort gave me some pleasure—yet I must admit that all of us are sometime takers of what's around—often called the "available given." Conflicts arise because some (of us) and more (of them) do not recognize that the best of givens are thrown around by well intentioned but innocent givers—milkmaids—babysitters—sophomores. The "them," in any case, are after debutants and don't usually socialize with "us"—which means that between "us and them" we don't share many givers. Nevertheless, now that days grow short, I suggest that we all should party more together—because the clashes of taste and belief, when expertly mixed and filtered, and appropriately served and shared—can make the best of givens for the takers on both sides.

But if one were to insist on being self (in) formed, and so venture out onto the dark mean streets alone—to join the thugs and hustlers—it would become evident that the give-and-take identifying our usual givers and takers, has another face to show. This can indeed be nasty. Yet I proclaim, when firmly out of mind, that I prefer to see the world that other way—however gross or dangerous it may seem—to the safety and familiarity that marks our every day—and gives us nothing in return but what we now have.

This alternative—embracing the farther deviance—is exciting but not easy. Reaching for freebies through the broken glass of a burning building is different from simple stealing. It has the problem of joining hostility with high purpose. It is the defining point for revolutionaries who need to show their own good reasons. You however, birthday boy—if you go that way—may become dead for no good reason. But I must also tell you, youngster—there are some-things worse: Mindless deviance is a lesser danger to the soul than is the loss of a moment of love—when on a passing ship, far from home—where the just met offers you the first taste of her body and high substance—and then the call sounds: "All visitors ashore!" You are left standing empty on the dock—in the sun of early afternoon—pale and still priapic—without even the comfort of good reasons.

I must trace this intersection of skepticisms—my dislike of a good and sober life crossing my dislike of heedless danger—to the duplicities of the gods who made me. They are the old ones, you know, those who have a pre-classic sense of humor. They are (I have researched it) the goatish, smart-ass gods who specialize in peculiarities such as mine. They gave me my given. I do freely what they know will follow from what they gave me. However, looking at how I stand in my own time—my early gods seem quite provincial when it comes to knowing what these-days people really want. But as gods go, they are good-gods, and they do—although I am not sure—(one can never be sure about the gods) what is needed, eternally speaking—and for my time of life—to keep me as richly divided as I am.

My secular friends tell me– as is a commonplace in urban circles— that there is a more contemporary way to adjudicate between the virtues and the vices of a life than by simply dividing them—and seeing which last longer. The gods could, e.g., have given me a life that does not sway onto one or the other side of the teeter-totter of living—so that, in my course of days, I could make a good show of maintaining a balance (highly prized in both ancient Greece and old New York) between skepticism and ambition. So why not, my friends say, ask your gods for a review of your current status?

Be careful, Lucian. Think twice about petitioning the gods to review their decision—remember the old warning about getting what you want. Consider instead: The one side—a life that is devoted to the anxieties which, as you age, crumble into an inert but comfortable skepticism, is a much admired role in academic circles. But on the other hand, laughing-all-the-way (which is the other side)—gets tire-some as one grows old. However, maintaining a measure between them is harder than it seems: Who now can adhere to the Golden Mean?

>How can the Main-Man go to town,
>long hairs growing out of ears and nose,
>slightly weaving on his crooked toes,
>and in that crumpled dressing gown?

>He's already got his tenure done.
>But still, he won't have fun.
>Do you think he remembers Rosebud?
>How she talked him in and teased him out—
>what with her pointy nose and insouciant pout?

>Others needed father figures in their time.
>You liked to look at girls.
>Never fear!
>You'll find a fragrant petal in your later years.
>But we both now know:
>Acerbic, anorexic, aggravating women will not do.
>Nor can you do enough for them.
>Because
>Beyond the single-minded rosebuds of your time,
>you craved the many-petal mount of Venus.

I suggest that before you leap across the sad remnants of winey flotsam, to the shore of sobriety and firm belief—realize that this second option also has its problems: The practical ambition of belief—whose tactics are meant to seamlessly integrate the where when and how into good hard manna—is too self-seeking for someone discontinuous as you. But if you were to choose that way—if for no better reason than, in your late years, you still need admiration—you will spend those years imbibing too much nectar, trying to digest yesterday's ambrosia, and tripping on your nose while sniffing at the dewy effluence of a young and winged goddess—who just flew back to heaven. This scenario can be long drawn-out, or too short—but never just right. It may well explain the yearning by self-proclaimed sinners for the oblivion of the lower brimstone pit: Stoke the coals if necessary—but no more happiness!

Actually, the gods don't much care which option you choose. Gods, as you may have noticed, do not, except in cryptic ways reveal why things are as they are—or whether what they do is always for the best—or who started it in the first place. The gods are the last ones that you want to ask about the given—when they have already given you (without your asking) what you are.

Even if the gods were willing to show you the small print in the Divine Plan, you had best not demand it of them. There may be better strategies: Gods are not good at dialogue—they seem to prefer, as Socrates sourly noted, unremitting praise and frequent festivals in their honor. If so—if that's what gods really want—why then would they bother with such an unlikely supplicant as you?

I must agree. The gods could have very well left me alone to make me real all by myself. With my given talents, I could have made a proper plan for me: All I would need to get started is a tabula-rasa for the future (no genetic limitations) and a cornucopia of possibilities to pick from (no material limits)—and then combine what I choose (combining is the hard part) into me as paragon. Additionally (and importantly) I would need something like Nietzsche's vehicle of the "Eternal Return," so that I could fashion both my past and future out of the accruing wisdom of my "now." Then, I could do without a guide to lead me through the perils of the choices I have made.

But in truth, it might be that neither the gods nor I are responsible for what I was and will become. Perhaps there are cosmic reasons, configured in that realm beyond the heavens, inscrutable to anyone I know or can imagine—for why I am as I am today. Such reasons will not out until all is done and gone—and that, you know, is long after everything has been said. Becoming is the antithesis to the given because it never ends—while the given has trouble making itself acceptable in circles where it is offered because its origins are in doubt.

But for now, I think it uncivil to blame my division on the gods. It comes to a class-distinction. They imbibe their nectar on high—while I am divided lower down. They live, as gods will do, in the best places on the largest hills of heaven, while occasionally peering at the cheap saloons in the lower parts of Brooklyn—my place of origin. But gods are good dissemblers. All they actually have is attitude, eternal livers, nectar and ambrosia made fresh by never-aging nymphs, and an unlimited supply of sacred events they give to us to celebrate. Not much.

Even this may change: The gods no longer seem capable of making any one thing—even me—into another. In both heaven and earth there are now laws about changing things too much. Then too: Secular reasons for my condition, such as evoking my rotten childhood, are now no more plausible than is the godly silence about my fondness for excess. Everyone I knew back then had a rotten childhood—yet we all went our different ways. So maybe I should tell more stories instead of looking for other reasons for my life.

XIV

MEMORIES

I REMEMBER, WHENEVER I caught a bad cold as a child, I was put to bed and given a potion of tea-honey-and rye whiskey to drink. Soon, I began to sweat and told my mother I felt better, and she would smell me, laugh—one of the few times I saw her happy—and let me cure myself into the night. Later, in my high-school days, there were times, at parties to which I sometimes was invited—when I began to feel soul-sick. I would then fasten onto the liquor bar, and soon I would not have to face the prospect of leaving with a girl I want to know.

College was salvation. The only possibility for me was Brooklyn College—a branch of the, then free, City University of New York. It wasn't easy to get in. One had to take a five-hour exam—all multiple-choice fill-ins that tested you from ancient history to beginning calculus.

I returned home—and we waited, my mother and I. Other kids in the neighborhood began to get acceptance letters—but none came for me. She could sense the Schadenfreude in the other mothers: "Your poor Polish kid is just dumb!" Then a letter came that said I was denied acceptance because I didn't take the test. "What? What? But I did!" So the next day, early, I went back to Brooklyn College and waited in line at the registrar's office. When my turn came, I exploded in descriptions, narratives, and demurrals—to plead for a place in the land of the living. The lady in the cage (she reminded me of the mothers in the Jewish cub scout group to which I once belonged) looked it up. She hesitated, looked further, and then she laughed. "They thought your name—Lucian—was a girl's name, so they put your test scores in with the girls. But there was nothing in the file of the rest of you. Wait, I'll find it. My, you did score high—and you did well in high school too! OK—you're in. We'll send an acceptance letter in the mail."

MEMORIES

I came back to where we lived—our apartment was a walk-up on the fourth floor. "Ma"—I shouted. She looked out of the window. "Ma—they thought I was a girl. It's all right now—I'm in." She shouted back—asking me if I was telling the truth—a suspicious love—but she knew this time. She then put on her best coat and walked around the neighborhood, telling all the women about the sexual mix-up now rectified, that would admit her smart son into college. "Yes—they thought he was a girl!" When she returned, she told me—with a bitter laugh—that the other mothers were not happy with the news. She died soon after.

My first class in college began with a tall, somewhat reticent, but well-spoken person who said: I am Professor De-Charms and I welcome you here, and I hope that you will have good times and also learn a lot during you stay. These were not his exact words—I don't remember—but I do remember being impressed by the civility—the sheer niceness—of his manner. Maybe hostility and shouting and hiding-out isn't all there is.

But the gap between being educated and coming from another world was difficult for me to bridge. There was a curriculum of sorts—but it was very democratic. The variety of choices was bewildering—it was again like being the little kid in the candy store. All beginning students were enrolled as English majors until they found their actual interest. So I took classes and dropped classes—the slightest irritation seemed to turn me off. My interests changed daily and I prowled the corridors looking for a clue as to what I would be when I finished college—more distantly, when I grew up.

A major distraction to this pursuit of vocation was my discovery of the seedy side of Greenwich Village—before its time of gentrification. I fell in with some bizarre teenagers from other boroughs, and we pooled our meager money and rented a loft on the bowery—a place to catch a dream for ten dollars each a month. There were five of us, and three actually lived there—in that gloomy, heatless, heartless, filthy rectangle—full time. I lived part time in Brooklyn with my aunt and uncle—where I could bathe and eat—and stay in school. Despite all the Bohemian airs, I came to dislike my village friends—actually, I was afraid that their willful fecklessness, disdain for education, interest in skullduggery, would also become my pattern. My vein of propriety was hidden in those days—but it was there.

So I stayed in school and found a course of study that balanced fragmentation and high purpose—art. Before that, I had tried anything that fed a fantasy: poetry, languages, literature—but none lasted. In those days, the study of art was still peripheral in the college curriculum—tucked away on the fifth floor of a minor building. It was called "Design" in order to qualify as a serious study for the City University of New York—"Art" wouldn't (historically) do. The Renaissance had long ago resolved the identity conflict between "artist" and "artisan"—but the news hadn't reached Brooklyn yet. The art faculty, in the main, cared nothing about commercial design, but were not yet (although some would become) heroes of the New York School. The chair was a harried man who had once studied with Moholy-Nagy at the Chicago Bauhaus—but couldn't quite convince his Brooklyn peers of the importance of that part of history or theory. The faculty consisted of serious artists—but none crazy enough to stake everything on the dicey throw of fame or oblivion. Instead, they used the easy stability of teaching to remain committed, without the need for histrionics, to their work. Good show, I thought—this is exactly what I want to do. My teachers soon became familiars. They needed young disciples—for their self-respect of course—but also to share their beliefs. What they believed was of an intensity that bewildered me—about peace, justice, social equality, progress, fame and love—all brought together through the agency of abstract art. This did not make sense—but it was a first good reason for me to look hard at history—as a way of making sense.

I had wandered into the department without having enrolled. Harry, my first guru, looked at my trespass and said that's fine as long as you work— I'll take care of the formalities. Although he never did specify the work at issue, I became an artist by smelling out—like an ambitious ferret—any clue to what "work" was really like. I made some decent abstractions just days after I had learned the word. In the evenings I followed my teachers to the artists' bars, where, pleased by my interest in their wayward doctrines, they bought me drinks. They drank an awful lot—I was awed at the rate of glasses being emptied, but I did not understand the need for all that drinking, nor for the nasty incoherence that followed. Surely, what they had was good enough—beautiful wives of just that perfect age, younger girlfriends too, a steady job with lots of free time, and an established presence in that magical realm—the art-world.

I finished college reluctantly—the umbilical had been quite nourishing. But it was the time of the Korean war—and I was drafted (into the Marines!) and eventually stationed in North Carolina. I was classified as—of all things!—a rifle-instructor. After some months, I met a Sergeant Pavonne, who was bright, Hispanic and gay, and also from New York—he was a rare romantic in the midst of dour and sullen Marines. Although he

MEMORIES

had enlisted, his optimism about Puerto Rico's affinity with America soon evaporated, and he, as I, waited for the day of discharge. When we could afford it, we frequented a pizza bar where the waitress was Hispanic. Pavonne extolled my virtues to her in Spanish and we drank rounds of beer. He wanted, I think, to see us both in bed, and then perhaps, crawl in to join us. The waitress—hirsute and beautiful—was married to a master sergeant she had met while he was on maneuvers in Puerto Rico. She had been working ever since to help provide for his bar bills and their three kids. Oh, she could have slept with me; perhaps she wanted to—or perhaps she thought that I, like Pavonne, was gay. I don't think she cared either way—it would, at least, have been a change from the frontal tactics of her hairy brute.

But she knew that I was a penniless private with college smarts, just waiting to get back to New York and my own freedom. Whatever else happened, she knew—and she was right—that I would do nothing that could take her and her kids to a better place. It was not my war—but in memory, it was a battle I had lost.

For artists in post-war New York, as an old painter described it to me, drinking is an occupational hazard. When I got back (it was 1955) there was success in the air—and the exuberance in the artists' bars, measured in decibels and drink, increased nightly as the latest news of shows, sales, and imminent immortality, circulated through the fumes and noise of evening. By that time, the radical ideal of art as a tool of social betterment, and the romantic infatuation with art as evidence of a Romantic illness, had both gone out of fashion. There were great new expectations in the air—few yet on the ground. But the nightly gossip in your ear was about what happened at the parties to which, somehow, you had not been invited: Who bought what—and sold it to which museum? Where are the critics placing their bets? What's the bippy on the latest bed-swaps? Who? What, when and where? But never: Why? Well, Lucian—you missed all that—even as you in spirit were there.

What to do, then, when it's all around you—but you're not-yet (not-ever) in it? Trink-Trink-Trink my boy, and you maybe can act crazy enough to make the others think that you are enough arrived to be invited. You could, of course, have made better paintings—if only someone showed you how. You would have been better off in the Middle Ages. Then, you could commend the paintings you had laboriously learned to make, to God—who, in turn, might urge the Pope to consider you—to begin with, for a fresco in a minor chapel. Or you might have ended just painting draperies and secondary trees. There actually were many hopefuls in the Cedar Bar who would have been happy to do just that—if only there were someone to show them how. But with Duchamp and Warhol in alliance, and Ad Reinhardt brooding in a corner, the once clear light of succession—from apprentice, to journeyman, to master—grew too dim for anyone to see. We were all ships passing in the night. Some had compasses—others (like me) did not.

The mornings after these anxious rites-of-passage, with only three hours sleep, were brutal—especially when I had to teach an early class. My job as artist-teacher (which I liked) was to assure those innocents that if they do all that I assign them, they too will gain a place at the tables of the artist-bars, and will have a chance—a better one than even I—to dance the flame dance of success.

Years later, my uncertainties about what I could do to further my career (I cannot imagine what such "furthering" would come to now) primed my decision to move to the mid-west to run an art-school that needed to hear the latest news. I was unhappy in New York—but the community of wealthy Saint Louis art-lovers welcomed me as a messenger. Perhaps fearing that I would imprudently question their latest—perhaps too-hasty and unduly expensive acquisitions—they invited me to parties to educate me in their ways. The most marvelous foods and wines were served, better than I had ever tasted—and the latest art purchases, shown after the brandy and cigars—were praised in full slurred voice, and only "pro-forma" disparaged. Everyone there knew the limits on pooh-poohing the tastes of powerful others—I was there to learn—and the parties, as one rich and tattered beauty told me, was the best way, despite it all, that they continued to live.

The boy from Brooklyn, much flattered to be there, became, early on, a player in the Saint Louis arty set. The higher-players in that spectrum were mostly involved in banking, manufacture, and chemicals. I was there because, as a (hired) New York sophisticate, and now administrator of THE art school in town, I might have some say in issues that concerned them—what to buy, where to donate their money, and whether and by whom to have their portraits painted. Warhol scared them. Judd made them comfortable.

I soon discovered that parties celebrating fine art also celebrated fine flesh. Both art and flesh were vulnerable in their particulars to critical censure, but the art would endure by maintaining its place on neo-baronial walls, and the flesh, primed by the best that grape could offer, would seek its

MEMORIES

satisfaction in equally elegant surrounds—satin sheets and rich perfume, peek-a-boos and plastic surgery, a practiced litany of demurrers followed by the requisite screams of abandon. For a while, I was a contender.

Those days remain encapsulated—a cocoon of bright and dark within the muted greys that form my larger life. I don't much remember episodes, but I do remember sounds and colors, and the movements that accompanied them. Not much content—but a lot of imagery—a stable of performers who played different parts on different nights. Saturday night was the loveliest night of the week—everyone was fresh, flush, and wanting. Sunday nights were tinged by the grey of approaching secular ambition. Monday and Tuesday—especially for the women—were put aside for rest and recuperation. Thursday and Friday were still far away, what with their need for protocols for new intrigues. Then there was Wednesday night—the meeting point of past and future—a time for fulfilling promises, and completing actions left so rudely interrupted. Wednesday's colors are silver and light purple—in contrast to the gold and black of Saturday. Mondays and Tuesdays are a spotted mauve, and Sundays end with the deep cadmium red of satiation.

But however much I enjoyed all that, I had a different life inside. (Yes, I am a firm believer in "insides.") So, after a year or so—encouraged by a strange and bright philosopher—Richard Rudner by name—who bypassed my stature as "Art School Dean" to further develop his own vision of philosophy as an extended conversation—and suggested that I study philosophy. I, somewhat off-handedly, agreed. My continuing and growing interest surprised me. The thought came clearly—although I had not (as I remember) thought it before—that I really (and for a long time) had wanted to be educated. So I began to study philosophy while still running the art-school. I don't know why the university went along with this—perhaps because of some exotic idea about an intersection of cultures—perhaps because some thought it funny, and also thought that it and I wouldn't last—also perhaps because others thought that philosophy was even crazier than art. But unlike those others, I was not troubled by the evident discrepancies in roles because I had become obsessed. The word did spread. I remember a beauty of my frolic days asking: "Why on earth?" I also remember my answer: "I'm trying to get educated." It was as true a truth as I could drag up from inside. She looked at me once more—up and down—then quickly left. What all the rest would come to—she didn't care and I didn't know.

ISSUES AND FRAGMENTS

To retrace a bit: An old good painter, in the early days, once said to me: "Nobody has it made." "Nobody? Not even with what you, or even say, Picasso, have done?" "Nah, nobody." The mood for my understanding this needed liquor's dark embrace. The seeds of skepticism, carefully watered, were then more deeply implanted, and their incestuous dependence on alcohol became as evident as life reflected in a room of mirrors. I wondered: Do artists with messages need alcohol to mollify both their triumphs and their failures? Is anything ever enough to provide an antidote—an alternative—to their reaching? Can one think past the pain of histrionics in favor of the clear way required for a sober ambition? Would it be better if artistic ambition were directed at the idea of "Being"—a form of making which is an exposition of an independent value? I think so now. Success in art has depended on a historical ambition. The attempt to exemplify history through art is like the hope of constructing a future for truth through philosophy. Deviance and failure in such attempts is a proper part of the game—a goad to dissatisfaction and renewal.

But, for the individual artist, the adoption of a style, and its correlation with present art-making remains a mystery. Perseverance in this could simply be a matter of wayward genes that express themselves in current modes of fantasy. If too painful—diagnosis and pills should take care of it. A psychiatrist once said to me: All artists are wounded. Mann had it right—he sent the novices up the magic mountain to join the battle between the ills of creativity and the ordinariness of health—the best of the well got sick and died. That was then. Now: However insistent was the effort to civilize the creative urge, and enlist it in the common battle—it remains an independent value. One alternative is to provide explanations. Aesthetic deviance does seem medically vulnerable—but, then, we cannot show that the sickest are the best. So what's the point? Van Gogh was probably schizophrenic; Caravaggio was a genius, a pedophile, and a killer. But Rubens and Picasso lived long fulfilled lives. In recent times, the relationship between sickness and creativity has been glamorized. Pollock was a real-time super-boozer and died in a car-crash. Rothko, perhaps looking for an older lineage of the understanding he so needed, slit his wrists in a bathtub. Others, less famous, drank away their dreams in anonymity. But as explanations of their accomplishments, none of this will do. Non-artists behave pretty much the same.

Wait; wait. Read a little further; I will lighten up, I promise. Truth is, I often sidestep such explanations. I have had many dry periods and good reasons for them. For example, I now have a granddaughter who will grow into her maturity when the echoes of her grandfather's art-world are at most a historical curiosity. So, in celebration of her coming, I resolved to smash my cache of wine, pour it into the passing river—or use it to water unwanted plants. There is still time, I thought, to anticipate some romping with my grandchild, and I must be ready-steady for it all. Tone, gesture, cadence, and skill in romping, are best when all is crisp and clear and agile. Who wants to be a muttering stumbling old drunk—especially when the little one is watching?

"Well said," intones Beelzebub. (He's always there when you want him least.) "But consider: you will be stumbling when the time for romping comes—whether you are sober or not. And you have always been known as a mutterer—part of your academic manner." This hurts—but I argue in return (get thee to thy ice-floe, Satan)—that there is a matter of early imprinting: I fear that every time she thinks of me she'll remember the smell of cheap Chardonnay (a real soul-destroyer this). The Devil answers back (he abhors the notion of live guilt followed by a still-living repentance). "Who knows which of your many foibles your grand-daughter will remember you by—you do have quite a few, you know." Here I must agree with him: Whatever my nefarious habits, it would be best if I lived long enough to give her a lot of choices for remembering—and let her, over the years, work out which memories she makes a grandpa of.

The turn to sobriety is not, even in these Republican days, a guaranteed rite of passage to the good life. (Actually, Republicans like to drink—it's the taxes they don't like). For years, my desires have been larded with images that showed forth my expectations, and these images were so artfully wrought (I do, after all, have a good imagination and some skill) that they masked the futility and timidity involved in larding desires with graven images instead of satisfying them directly.

But I'm learning. For example: I prefer loving to it's describing. I still work a lot on describing—but afterwards I use a bladder of wine to mollify the anxiety of long afternoons of pure describing—with no love. Lately, I've tried, with some success, to bring the two together—doing and describing—in no particular semantic order: "bladder" gives way to "bottle"—"model" becomes "lover"—"canvas" expands to "terrain" (or, in my more aggressive moments—"arena.") The "art-world" becomes the "whole–world."

But, however named, these considerations make the evenings shorter than would the examination of conscience that may (or may not) lead to sobriety. The wine, at least, protects my nights from the anxiety of worldly goings-on. (Elections are now forever.) But you know, such protection is not reliable. It can be a double agent by allowing the intrusion into quiet ruminations about the renewal of self-love and accomplishment, by accusations that past works (my own unresolved ideas) "should by now be finished." (The locution "should"—like the Devil—always returns). By late morning, though, I am sufficiently clear to counter my sleeping scolds by deciding that I will not be a more severe critic of my efforts than either they or I deserve. After all, we've known each other, my efforts and I, wet and dry, for a long time now. The Devil is not needed.

I miss drinking most when I'm trying to be happy—strange—that's when one would think to need it least. When I drink alone I am sometimes happy—sometimes not—it depends on what, if anything, I feel I'm missing-out on. But of course, when I'm drinking with another, who also approaches her problems through a glass of winy promise and waiting despair, we can tell each other (after the requisite fumbling) how good it is to be together. This leads to the thought that if we extend the night into tomorrow night, there is a probable-certainty that tomorrow is bound to be even better than today. But today's penitents (we all are such) are not easily fooled by last night's happiness—come the dissecting light of morning. The memories of moon-beams reflecting off a thigh—are, after a while—not strong enough to counter the haze of the despair which lurks, timelessly, in the sweaty smells and squeaks of strangers' beds.

I can afford to scold myself this way—because essentially we like each other—me and I. But I have become wary of the other scolding voices that fulminate against my any chancy hope of combining variable flesh, decent wine, tasty food, good art and such other commendable stuff, into a casserole of (yes) transient happiness.

Used to be, the dry and pointy noses only carried on in back rooms and vacant auditoriums, singing their hymns and thumping out their beliefs. But now, with the electronic ease of messaging, they mount some serious opposition (would you have thought it) to the openness of living—an opposition that has moved from nostalgia for a virtuous past, to the old drum-roll of sectarian hatred:

> Burn, whip, shoot—emasculate, eviscerate.
> If not: Convert, deport, or kill them dead.
> Perverts, atheists, terrorists and socialists.
> Pluck-out their hair.
> Toss them out-of office.

MEMORIES

> Better:
> Sit them on a sharpened stake—
> planted in the middle of the square.

Counter-arguments to such monstrous beliefs have become weaker these days—because liberals still insist on being sensitive to the need for a flexible response when challenged. The most committed among us will offer cultural explanations for the calumniating directed at some or other identified face of sin, and—smiling—will wave back "hi-there" to the threats, hallelujahs and amen. To expand on the point: The more committed of liberals sometimes regard the slaughter of innocents in foreign lands as differences in belief (their country's business) or as historical changes in the direction of enthusiasm (the world's business). All this is in the name of freedom and its infinitely variable mandate.

Once, when "progress" (a variant of world-business) was in flower, the wiser of the old ones thought that polemics against skin-born pleasure would end—soon if not immediately. Later, seeing that the world-engine is slower on this score than first thought, the new wise ones accepted (naively as it turns out) the inclusion of local scolds as a broadening addition to our understanding of this our modern age. But inclusion, as we are painfully learning, does not satisfy the keepers of the road to righteousness—they want it all—and the battle is now joined. On the one hand, inerrant truth and dire punishment for disbelief. On the other hand, slogans offered in the marketplace that mask what we know and do not know, and vitiate what we should and should not do. We still offer polite conversation, picnics on the grass, and decision fudging as good governance—whatever the issues.

But none of this is for the born-again: "Truth"—capitalized and glorified—stupefied and militarized—is again winning the day, much as it did in those hard and painful times—of pogroms and inquisitions—when admitting to uncertainty was worth your skin. The latest gambit of this newest atavism—the fundamentalist attempt to retake our bodies—is to slather virtues rather than emollients onto skin. "Eat more spaghetti"—said the prelate to the novice with priapic problems. "Just say no"—says the power behind the throne. Believing that virtues travel from untouched skin to empty mind discourages the contrary belief that skin is for pleasure and mind is for wisdom. But a free dialogue between skin and mind is as important as the dialogues between skin and skin, and mind and mind. Such interplay (each in its own way)—is crucial, as I believe—for the requirements of the soul.

ISSUES AND FRAGMENTS

It is a question, now, of how slowly the world-as-progress can go and still, if at all, continue to move. The actuality of such movement, of course, is not an empirical matter, and thus cannot be recognized except from the timeless perspective of an eternal being. That, sad to say, is the perspective our local-holy-folks have taken as their own—the belief that the end of the world (or, more modestly, its reversal) will prove them right. But even countenancing such fantasies, if only for the sake of social even-handedness, is a weakness of aging radicals. It is a relativistic tic, a willingness to reconsider—for sophistic-academic reasons—ideologies that they should, and I do, abhor.

It's been awhile- I don't remember exactly—since I've slept concurrently with more than one woman. I miss that constellation—the sky seems emptier. But I don't confuse its disappearance with the recurring desire for a drink. I take it, rather, as a sign, not of the transience of lust, but of the remnants of my confusion about loving some one to the degree that, with only passing regrets, I will leave the others alone. It may be, then, that my cooled yearnings for new love experiences are not to be explained as the end of a long-time winey fling—but of a sufficient love. Drinking, as I believe, is not a causal agent of the urge to promiscuity—it is merely a supportive factor. The real-deal is harder to reach.

Desires for sex and drink may have little to do with each other or with happiness—which, when achieved in its quietude, should be the preferred alternative for those who no longer want to balance the rest. Neither can the insistence of these desires, when practiced to the detriment of happiness, be explained (I know; I've tried) by dredging up all those inadequacies for which they must be symptoms and substitutes. In varieties of non-western medicine, such disorders are thought to simply go away—if only one sits, chants, and waits long enough. I write and paint—that helps too—but I'm not looking for a cure. Desires—whether longings for the ineffable, or a liking for orgasm—are not, as I believe, illnesses or faults. They are basic ancient instruments that need practice to be played well.

To love one's self, despite it all, is a good mulch for whatever variety of life you early think to plant—even when later, you dig it up and plant another version you believe will give you better blossoms. When you are dead and gone, the continued blooming of your plants provides a growing screen of information about your self. This is even more valuable than when you were alive—because, then, you probably didn't appreciate flowers as you do now that you are dead.

MEMORIES

In the early years, when invective and profligacy were daily companions, stamina was required to ride out the dry and painful times. The understanding that such stamina was a portent of self-love came later—when introspection became a practiced defense against the world—a shield that gave you time to hide from the grosser actions of life—yours and theirs. One gets little rest when one is young. The older ones, however, are constant in their peering—trying to determine whether you—fledgling—will rise or fall—be ground into the local hamburger, or (even worse) fly to a point they cannot reach—and make them hope, against their finer instincts, that you will fall. Someday, the better of the elders you have met will plan an outing. They will suppose, because of expected gratitude for their early support and counsel, that you will take them with you on a safe flight to the latest newness. But before you realize—just when you're beginning to like them—you might find that you are coming to be like them. The old ones—even the smarter ones—want the future to be a more tasteful embellishment on what they already have.

So be wary, youngster, of the old. They are (in the main) so planted in the convenient mix of duty, greed, and "enlightened self-interest," that they will tell you—as a justification for their sags and wrinkles—that they have finally transcended the need for self-love—and so, have become (for a mere pittance) a source of self-less nurture. Don't believe it! They have simply turned their needs onto you—and they see you as an instrument for extending their span: You are young, fairly strong—an unformed vessel, true—but (and they can be shrewd) one that has value if you work out as they wager. Oh, don't accuse me of "age-ism." I know others, real old ones, who aren't at all like that. Some, in fact, remain obsessed with their own talents and are brim-full of self-love—which occasionally spills out and gives good water—clean fresh water—gin-clear—to the young. I'm like that.

XV

QUALITIES OF PEOPLE I HATE

(Listed in no special order—
To be elaborated on below)

Parsimonious—Frugal—Abstemious—
Celibate—Lecherous—Porno-phobic—
Dry mouths—Parched souls—Shallow pates—
Gossips—Denunciators—Pretenders—Believers

Parsimonious

I have a pocket full of dimes.
You can have one if you're good.
As regards your mother, sister, and your brother—
each can have a fine dime too if they behave—
or go with the nickel they've sinfully saved.

Frugal

Why should I give in to pleasure—
when privation pleases me better?
I enjoy looking down upon
my skinny knees and bony toes—
knowing that the powers that be,
afterwards will feed the best of me—
and praise my pointy nose.

QUALITIES OF PEOPLE I HATE

Abstemious

No thank you, not right now—
I've had too much already.
I would hate it if my figure grows
from early planar to balloonious.
I also hate it when at parties
they force fat food on me.
I really hate the thinking about eating
that persists when I am sleeping.

Celibate

No need to be molested—probed and penetrated—
when I could just as well have stayed at home.
And you, my brother, need not bewail
another night of erectile travail
when you, like me, could resort to
the privacy of your long clean fingernails.

Lecherous

Jump and pump on the available rump.
Don't seek directions even when she's talking—
make-do with what you know you have.
But remember—someone else will annotate
the frequency, ease, and volume of arousal.
And don't forget you didn't try with her—
(Why not?—she's clean and mean)—the
prevarications that one reads about.

ISSUES AND FRAGMENTS

Porno-phobic

I hate dirty pictures.
I despise the creeps who watch them.
What kinds of monsters make them
into seeming what in fact they are?
Watching others is the worst—
much worse than doing it to yourself—
which in-itself is bad enough.

Dry Mouths

Retentives have dry mouths.
They can't wet their lips to crack a smile.
The inverse shape of pouting is easier.
All the moisture stays inside.
Besides—
The eating of forbidden fruit needs liquidity—
much as banks do for investment.
The divestiture that follows
must go smoothly, and that needs
moisture too—don't you get it?

Parched Souls

Nulling winds can dry the soul
by evaporating the hope that mind
should transfer to the body—if only
we could believe that death is not a sting.
But no oasis can yet be found.
The blowing sands are unremitting
in covering the eyes and mind
with cynical gritting—
leaving ears and nostrils as the only space
the desiccated soul has left
to find a proper place past living.

QUALITIES OF PEOPLE I HATE

Shallow Pates

Kant calls them shallow-pates—
the ones who can't distinguish between
categorical and hypothetical
grounds of acts performed—either
for the sake of duty, or conversely,
for the satisfaction of an itch.
I, however, consider it a duty
to respond to my body's imperative
that I dispassionately scratch.

Calumniators

I often want to smack a friend who tells
others how I comb my hair—
or reveals the source of my despair
about missing out when truth and beauty
made open love—to the cheers of rabble—
celebrating the waftings of their pubic hair.
Look and listen!
First the whispers—and then a crying-out.
I missed it all—and all because I
don't like making love in public places.

Denunciators

J'accuse—all of you who abrogate the rules
of canon law and just plain decency.
Custom has it that we break you on the rack—
but that might hurt your back.
None-the-less, you must suffer
our appropriately issued penalty.
This to show others of your kind that
profligacy will always find a snitch
who pretends to be a noon-time snack.

ISSUES AND FRAGMENTS

Pretenders

Life was good when there were thrones
for pretending to.
Chances are you might get one—
if you pretend hard enough.
Watch out, though, for rightful kings
whose grandfathers
were themselves pretenders.
Their heirs will break your bones
before you can write your name
upon the palace gate.

Believers

Don't make-believe. Believe in God.
True belief is never false belief.
But there is an X someone believes.
And a Y believed by hostile others.
What, then, to do when believing is made
by people but unmade by rattlesnakes?
Nonetheless.
We'll band together and say out-loud:
This is what we all believe—
because we're the only true-believers
within the cosmos, and we will make
the most of what we have around us.
So listen hard!

XVI

A DIFFERENT PASSAGE

I MAY BE ON the mantel in a can by the time you're reading this. It is not that I'm watching you and listening (or touching, smelling, tasting) to see if you are still soft and lithe and lissome—as you were the day before the day I died—some middle time that occurred a good while after I was born.

You can see I now have no sense in general, and none with which to reciprocate—to offer explanations, cast aspersions, bring you flowers—and still refuse—as once I did—to counter everyday illusions with disbelief, ferocity or fright. This is especially true, now that the season's ended and the weather is still warm enough to support the sounds of birds. No—I'm not sorry that I don't hear them. "Sorry" is not an issue where I am. Nor am I sorry that I can't romp and rave and reminisce—as once (this last was closer to the end) you bravely bore—it was the price for—and I hope it will turn out to be—some part of your life's content.

I, in turn, am no more content than I am sorry—for the same reason—no thinking of regret or contentment here—in the same way that being sorry is sequestered for the living. But there still is something here that "moves"—as the writing you are reading proceeds from word to paragraph to sense (your sense—not now the same as mine). You are right to consider this a ploy—a border dispute—to write my death into your life while it may be that I'm still alive. But, believe me—It might as well be that I'm dead by now. So I too am right—for writings have their own time and give their own examples of what it is to be alive or dead. These examples are not mine—I have always insisted that art is not dependent on the artist. To be read is for a writing to be on its own—and it must suffer the consequences: It may be said (of it) that it combines the "nicely nuanced" together with the "out of date," and, occasionally drops down to the "poorly conceived." But, a "writing" (I can't speak for all—only the ones enough like mine) does not suffer the tenderness of life. Writings are not touchy. Rather, they evoke times of memory and anticipation—those that skip actual life by grasping linearity by the throat and making it into times that have no historical direction, expressive urgency, or social insistence. That these are times that then split into fragments—should not be forgotten. For these fragments—in their coming together and going apart—are the life we have when dead. It may be that you never were in my time of life—but only in my time of writing. Sorry if I misled you about the actuality thing. As I have said—actuality is for the present sense. I, in contrast (if dead) am now into reality—which does not have the "when and where" of ordinary time and place. My time (if I am where I say I am) has neither sense nor tense. Yet, I am impressed (as only the dead can be) by the scope of infinite (if impersonal) time, and the range of indefinite (if capricious) memory—which provide the solaces for where I am. My, it's a large place here—larger than life. How I know this I can't tell you—it's like the question of what makes the intelligible possible—it is unanswerable (even through latter-day brain dissection)—but it's a good question to have around.

To be "at all times, everywhere" is the ultimate ambition. (Just remember, youngster—you are, even in the limit of your time, a member of the "all-of-us"). But this ambition is not an attribute of yours or mine—for if it were, there would have to be other attributes—designating different ambitions—and then we're back to actuality. Rather, this particular ambition consists of a supposing—better, a metaphysically regulated flight—that if this ambition were realized—if you could be everywhere at all times—or, more modestly, a somewhere at a time of your choosing—why, this could be serve as a description of "God!" Would you like to be God?

Such a grand ambition (to be everywhere at all times) is certainly God-like, in that it must hold as well for past and future. It can also serve as a definition of immortality. Of course, there are many levels of ambition, and this post-life variant should not be confused with mundane life-ambitions—such as the desire for dancing girls, his-and her Porsches, or a castle in Spain. The grandest ambitions—it is said—are suffered by the lesser gods. Indeed, they reach for them when things are not going well—when other gods—younger, stronger—show up, and insist on negotiations to divide the claims of the older gods to eternal spoils. When agreement is reached—some gods retreat to treasures of the past, others will opt for the riches of the future. Consider this when you want to be a god.

A DIFFERENT PASSAGE

I am not a god (as you well know) but I dream a lot—and now that I'm timeless, my dreams are larger than when I was still shuffling in the linear mode, back on the afore-said mortal coil. But if I were a god, I could make all things, now alternatively geometric and chaotic, into a total harmony. Then, I would know the up and down, the in and out, front and back—even the beginning and the end. Why—I could then make the world—indeed, the cosmos—better than it was when I was actually still alive. Well, maybe the gods will read this, enlist me—or do the better thing themselves. But I doubt it: gods are much like members of congress—they only want your vote. Does this sound cynical? Sorry—I should (where I am) be past all that. But every now and then (that phrase, you know, is just a metaphor around these parts) I still get angry.

> Being mad makes me feel like the raw Kielbasa
> that is floating in my lower pit of bile—
> waiting for its transformation into shit.
> This happens when others are unconditionally vile.

"Others?" What others? Is this another of your blown-up universals? All the others you know? All the others you hate? All others who have ever lived? All possible others? No—no. I only designate those others I once hated, and still do—except I don't see them any longer. One nice thing about this place is that such people are not here. Here, we are attuned to the one's we love.

But I do remember the others. If you look at my notes, you will find them listed and succinctly described. I am not a violent man (I used to wish I were)—so I will not emulate my adversaries—and say: "shoot them, kill them, grind them into dust." They deserve it, certainly—not only because they were bad as such—but also because they paid me no attention. This latter is worse than being calumniated, denigrated, undervalued, dis-invited to the year's "most-prominent-parties." But from where I am, I no longer think them ill. Times have changed in after-life. We saved-elite no longer sit on marble parapets listening to the screams wafting up from down below. Bad taste, now. Good thing, though—because I don't know whether I'd be here or there—that is, if the old customs were still in full and flaming force.

Yet (pro-forma) I hate those others still. Because I'm better—yes!—at doing what I do than the me they talk about. Actually, they didn't talk enough about me. Didn't know—they—what to say—eh? But I must be fair. What could they say when they didn't know me—as I do? My fault, I suppose. (It always is).

ISSUES AND FRAGMENTS

It's strange here. I remember feeling this or that about this and that—but now that I'm here, I don't feel like either this or that- one just doesn't. Also, I don't know whether here (if that makes sense) is up or down—and I don't ask now. One just doesn't. There are others—as I remember them—who might ask me what I'm doing here. I won't tell them. One just doesn't. They'll have to read my books.

I don't know
and I don't care.
I no longer have to
put on glasses,
nor look for
underwear.

Really, one doesn't wear anything here. There might be some such—robes, loin-cloths, penitential rags—to be put on. But I don't know—haven't looked—it's optional. Anything "to do–to be–or have–or want" is a memory of things already done—nothing new here. There is nothing "to regret"—nothing "to wish." As regards vocation, it's better here to dream. In dreams, something real—if only a passing wisp—a flimsy figment—a remembered sound—can be found. But nothing that is actual—is acceptable.

I'm not saying death is (like) a dream—but I'm not saying it isn't (like one) either. Let me tell you how it really (but not actually) is. You see, there are no contraries when you die. If you want action—don't die—go elsewhere. Here, all action—tension, hesitation, hoping, fearing, sulking, moping—disputation, bifurcation, assignation, constipation, fornication—ends. And with this ending, all goads to rethinking or redoing end as well. So the variety in dreams that occurs after death lacks the component of ambivalence or anxiety. There is no incessant climbing of a cliff, or getting lost in an unfriendly town, or voicing the same old entreaties to a changing cast. None of that, not here! Instead, dreams of the dead grow upon the ones compiled when dreams were still alive. Anxiety is replaced by embellishment—ambivalence by elaboration—the sneaky swerves in actual time by a central cosmic flowering. It's not bad at all—try it—you may like it. Here, you don't go to anywhere; you build on what you bring along; your little flower joins with the big blooming (just mentioned) of the cosmos. As the passing thug once said to me—when I was kissing Heidi on Delancy Street: "Way to go!"

A DIFFERENT PASSAGE

There is a moral in this story. There is a moral in every story—but most go unheeded. Good thing! I dislike morals. But as my story is being read by you and yours, its moral should be heeded: If there is an afterdeath—then it should have the character of everything you bring to it from life. This has to do with your ability—in life—to remain incomplete.

If you're of the kind to know the meaning of it all at an early age, and you hold to that same meaning until you die, you'll not get corroboration here. You won't even get here—there are other places. But then, for you, death will at best be boring—at worst, nothing. If, however, you are spotted walking on the road—with songs unsung, manuscripts in progress, paintings that need repainting, a ledger of past and present loves—then you'll (in a different sense of "you") continue having rich and fecund dreams—all working on the fragments you have brought with you—but there will be nothing of your doing in this that's new. That's the way it is here—and if it so suits you (you do look as if you were a much belabored living thing who, nevertheless, assiduously protected a vision of its soul) why eternity will be (for you) an infinity of communal story-telling about the many different ways a soul is found—and the many reasons it needs protection.

XVII

ETERNITY

ETERNITY, WHEN YOU THINK about it, is a big problem. You can find it in the veins of a leaf, and it shows (on a larger scale) in the birth and death of nations. It might be heard in a moan of low delight—or in the slurp of wine that commemorates the last bite of a well-cooked steak. There is some eternity in the sound of reading, and more in listening to the wisdom of a demented friend (he is already there).

Eternity does indeed have many sounds—but it is not to be heard in the supplication of innocents or lamentations of the guilty. Such sounds are not too faint to hear—but no one listens. Neither does eternity sound in the songs commemorating the deaths of millions, nor in the arguments of those whose pensions have been cut—no one wants to listen. Yet, all these have a part to sing in the sound of eternity.

'Eternity' is a word that came up in middle language. It is a dreadful word for the living. We keep it because we are afraid of it. It reminds us of the shortness of our span. And it asks us why—with all we have been given—why we all die. Must we all die? Is that a "given" too? Whoever gave this given must be powerful—for it seems to work in every case. 'Death' is another familiar word in our language. It is more straightforward than is 'eternity.' It refers to all of us, to slaughtered animals, murder victims, to the landscaped mounds of buried soldiers, and to inhabitants of old-age homes. It also has a place for entry in a ledger.

The "death of consciousness," however, is not a question for eternity—(not yet, anyway). It is a question we must individually ask—because all sorts of mental functions will go on after yours and mine are over. Some of these we now call consciousness, others haven't shown up yet to claim a name. (Do you really think we're the end of the evolutionary line)?

ETERNITY

Concerning my consciousness: I won't too much miss (the reflective awareness of) raw sex, tender breezes, or good wine after I am dead. But I will miss some other aspects of my consciousness—The about-ness that we write of, the reciprocity of mutual awareness, fond memories and future fears. All this is absurd, of course—as if missing without awareness were at all possible. But then, as regards consciousness, death is impossible. Thinking about dying, or being dead and not thinking—is not the same as being dead and thinking.

The prospect of not thinking is why I'm writing this story about after death. I'm alive while writing this—so there must be some other reason for supposing (not pretending) that a dead Lucian is writing this. You may well reproach me for trickery, moribundery—worse: for talking affectionately about death when still alive. You're right. I have spoiled enjoyment of the Holiday Feast by suggesting that the smell of ripe cheese evokes a corpse, or that red wine looks like blood when spilled upon a white dress, or that some in the morning look like death (twice) warmed over. Sorry I am—yes—but not about the feathers ruffled on the breasts of the otherwise complacent or inattentive. I regret the strain I've laid upon the rules that guide our intimacy.

Why do I subject you—you who are my loves—to the saga of my no longer being? And worse—gussy it up with self-seeking descriptions of an afterworld where I would really like to be—but actually don't believe that such will ever be? Well, as you expected—I have excuses: The actual world is now for us and later not for us. But I do believe that thinking of death while living is a way of contrasting (while alive) the actual world to the real world of after-death. Thinking this way changes the notion of time—it relieves us of our selves; it modifies the fear of inevitability; it connects generations in a common cause. This is not the cause of actual life—with all those good things like peace and love. Rather, it is the cause of the imponderables that consciousness permits—the realities before being born and after dying, and the astonishing fact that, as the man said, "there is something rather than nothing"—that we are here at all.

In other circumstances, it is usual to ask—about such conundrums—why we are asking. But "Why"—this word ringing like an accusatory bell since the beginning of time—is the most slippery word in language. It never fully reveals its asker. It often pretends there is no asker—only the question—Why? Why? It presents itself as the largest question of them all—the one that interrogates the source and consequences of being—the question that is independent of its asker's motives. But you—my abstract but inveterate asker, sneaky interloper to my story—my "why" you cannot hide from. Once you have been spotted, you are obligated to answer to some version (my own, perhaps—or yours) of the question "why." This obligation is not caused by your asking (you have your own reasons)—but it is a reminder of the limits of our living. The answers to the question "why?"—given by those who are bemused enough to make the effort—do not come from the compendium of daily living, which can only show the art of having learned to evade answering painful and prolix questions. The urge to answer comes from another source: Every living moves toward a hiatus, and consciousness addresses this realization through the question "why." The realization carries with it the obligation to answer.

"Obligation," in certain respects, is more immediate than "why." It is more visceral yet more threatening—and it has the additional problem of direction. To whom are we obligated? Is it to our selves, our loved ones, our nation, the world, the Cosmos, to God—or to nothing? (Skeptics should enjoy the juiciness of "an obligation to nothing.")

Heidegger identifies "that" as the key to primary philosophical wonderment—that there is something rather than nothing. But "that" as contrasted to "why" does not give us a salient question. It is not directed to any source of answer—not even to a self. Rather, it is the existential prime—the thought that shows itself as first consciousness before the recognition even of a self. It is wonderment—pure—at the coming of the first experience. But the "that," however primary, is passive. It stays in place—however fast or infinite place may be. "That" avoids the smallest urge toward the reflection that could reveal a life.

So, living still, I prefer the "why"—the question that follows "that." "Why that?" Its potential for generating opposites—conflicting answers—is also a first harbinger in our consciousness of "freedom." We are free to choose—although, as Kant says—we cannot know why we are free. This indicates the limits of reflection—the (so-to-speak) dispassionate silence of eternity. But my "why" also shows the enduring residue of my Romanticism—and is attested to by the (ongoing) music of the spheres. (Can't you hear it)? Divided as I am, however, the sound that confounds my silence often takes other forms. Sometime, I hear it as a howl—mostly at night—when all that seemed right goes wrong. In my most fragile nights, it is the imperative of primary subjects of past howls that provides the authority, and content, of bad dreams.

ETERNITY

Howling seeks no listeners and expects no answers—or so it says. (A question: If one wants to access another's dream—would it be better to look-in or listen-to?) For me, a bit of either is fine—it depends on place, and age, and who the dreamer is. But such dreams of mine as generate my howl of "why" to a world I do not know the limits of—those dreams insist on being both shown and heard. They thereby mark their independence of me—but not mine of them. The sounds emitted when I howl, evoke a wide scenario—a play (partial listing) of action, inertia, anxiety, hope and anticipation. My particular howling plays the lead in games I play when writing. The latest text is always the one that you are reading. It is the one that demands your attention, and yet asks (like now) if you are still game to go along.

You can ask for help, of course. I'm sure you'll find some who are willing to help you through the scary parts. They'll also tell you stories about how I live between the writings—but these stories often lie. Actually—enlisting help could take us into some turgid metaphysics denser than the books I write—or to some nasty old-time acrimony. So I'd prefer that you go it alone; dream along with what you read of me, and find the passages that scratch the earth and look beyond the heavens. These are the places that connect the living with the dead through the stories we share.

XVIII

THE PLACE FOR EVERYONE

It's there.
That place where the quick and the dead
can both abide and share.
Looking for it is as good as listening to it,
but thinking of it is the best.
Horrific, though,
to think that consciousness
gives way to putrefaction.
But that's the way it goes.
Unless
We separate the body from its script
and give the latter eternal life—
so long as it doesn't hope
to change the world it's left—
the one where ignorance
beds down with innocence—
and so ends in becoming rot.

Let me tell you about this other place—
the place where I'm now at.
It's an empty place—although
there are others there.
The dead don't congregate,
only the living do.
For the living hope that
custom will continue

THE PLACE FOR EVERYONE

to make the dying
just like living—only better.
Because death, as we must accept—
moves slower.

The cost of dying is atrocious—
but once you're done it must be done.
And others, bless their hearts,
will have to pay—just
when memories of the dear departed
begin to go astray.

You can't take it with you—as you know.
But why, he cried, do I have to go?
So what is it you don't know?
Oh—that.

XIX

LIFE AND DEATH

A PLACE CAN BE known by its absence of events as well as their profusion. Where I'm at is not eventful. It has the aura and memory of events—but nothing actually happens. This is quite appropriate—as everything that was to happen, has already happened. There are—as I mean to tell you—others of my kind around. We may even—some of us—have known each other back then—when things still changed and so made events—which could very well, as everything in life, have included you and me. But there is nothing further in our tales for us to make a change. All is forgiven—nothing is forgotten. The memories that are our final sense—however generous or thin—can have no adding-to. That's the rule here: Nothing more—make do now and forever with what you scraped together when back there and then. This does seem harsh—but it's a lesson, often too late given—about the danger of small-stuff engorging containers beyond capacity—a late critique of affluence, one might say. But think instead of when you stuff potato-salad into take-out boxes in the local super-market. If you don't think a full box is enough—take some wings along—you'll be hungry later, and there's nothing worse than spending eternity with a grumbling in your stomach.

We don't share here—no matter what—it's against the rules. The reason, however, for this legislation is a good one. It is a matter of finding time, sharing time, and one's own time. These are like the "stages of man" (although women are here too)—each has a purpose in the flow. But when the last of the three is done, the subject of what you are shows up. It turns out to be what you have brought together to (finally) make your stages all convene into yourself. You'll be chewing on that one for a while—the longest while there is. That the time before-you has no beginning should concern you less—you came later—although you may meet some forbears

LIFE AND DEATH

and suggest they take blame for what you turned out to be. But the time after-you should concern you more—for (if I am right) neither of you has an end. This situation requires looking at the resources you've brought along to shape the "after" as you begin your endlessness. Have you ever dreamt about what never ends? Did you, when awake, continue to make love after repetition became too repetitive? Have you kept on painting, writing, singing optimistic songs—after what you've already done leaves you no place to sit or stand?

Don't fret—it's no longer a battle for survival in the afterlife. It goes more like this: Remember back when you were stuck in a small town because your car broke down? It first seemed like a stretch of total emptiness—intolerable to a febrile spirit like your self. But as you grew older (in a matter of hours) you began to look at the resources you brought with you—and you thought to show them to the others also stuck in their own broken time: They liked them just fine. Then, you found that you could relish the fragrance of fried chicken, watch the commercials on the TV in the daytime, take a slow walk along the broken streets, and talk earnestly with the father (avoiding the mother) of the large family in the next cabin who had just finished their yearly week's vacation. As with exile, deportation, or a broken timing-belt, creativity continues in the afterlife—but it's of a special kind. It shows itself in the novelty of re-collection—in a play of memory's willingness to re-arrange the essence of ones-self.

I make a distinction between the concepts of "end" and "limit"—a distinction that continues past the silence that protects the unity of rationality. This shows itself when we say "the limits of life"—although we mean the "end" of actual living. The distinction here correlates with the other distinction I have proposed—between "actual" and "real"—where "actual" refers to the empirical world and the dynamics of physical change, and "real" refers to the world of human consciousness of memory and history—where the speculative construction of past and future extends the reality of an individual life into death. Simply put: When I die I actually am dead—it is the end of my physical life; but it is not the limit of my "real-life"—for this limit develops through the extensions of my lived life into the constellation of other lives.

Dying does not end the reality of life—whose limits are constructed (in past and future times) by the memories, affects and effects, of having lived. My death, to be sure, precludes my further contribution to this reality—but my previous interval, as someone living—contains the impact that my life will have on others. This impact shows in memory and the residue of actions—and it changes through the attention, forgetting, obliteration and reconstruction—given it by the living. But they, like we, will also die, and the reality of all-of-us continues to change accordingly. So I ask you: Is it not a comfort, within your now actual life, to know that you do not know the limits of your existence, and also know that these will continue on (expand or contract as you have wrought them) into the real life beyond your actual end.

In his novel, "Magister Ludi,"—or "The Bead Game" (1943), Hermann Hesse describes a late society that has become historically passive. Instead of living towards a future, it ritualizes all it has accumulated from the past into different patterns of completeness—multiple games of novelty within sameness. Creativity, here, is supplanted by memory—the abandoned future by the richness of the past. This is a metaphor for my society of afterlife. When alive, we try to bypass what hinders our living. After death, we seek to regain all that has happened when we were alive. The past is as infinite as the future—we can never know all of it. And those with no future, the dead—yet have all the past in which to situate—to be. But as the past (as with the future) is larger than any of its representations, new segments and scenarios continue to emerge—and, so, rearrangements form new games that include (some of) these emerging recollections. The living die—and provide the already dead with new memories of their common past—to be used as elaborations for the games they play.

The master of the game (Magister Ludi)—perhaps modeled after Plato's philosopher-king—is devoid of self-interest. But as a good administrator, he directs the game in the direction of universal coherence in order to confront the threat of irrationality and fragmentation. Actually, he is a somewhat strange fellow—a failed artist who becomes a de-facto realization of order, but is also somewhat of a voyeur. To control the game he must be acutely aware of the ubiquitous play of appetite, gratification and denial that motivate performers as they play their parts in the variations of each episode. As master, however, he must be implacable in maintaining rhythm and coherence. He must direct each played part of partial recall into an affirmation (if not confirmation) of total recall. Each game shows everything there is. The Bead-Game is thus a paradigm of optimism. But such a goal, even within the imposed constructivism of each game—remains an ideal. The master's mission in this regard is clear: The games must strive for a representation of the unrealized unity of the actual world

LIFE AND DEATH

But there is another history here—a less philosophical one: The master, after all, became ascendant in a time of worldly crisis—his proposal of "world-as-game" was important for understanding. He accepts the dual nature of art and reality—but also, the perverse seductions of unity. He must know that we do not ask of a Mandala whether it is more beautiful than the other—and so he must also realize that the games played are never won, lost, or ended. Performances change, but the game does not. This makes for difficult governance. Nevertheless, the celebration of (collective) memory as a form of life must continue—if we are to believe in transcending death. The game ends only when the living are no longer needed by the living. Then there is only slaughter to be introduced—the game repeats itself, as do animals in their sameness—and the reality of death becomes a bore.

Hesse wrote in a Romantic time, and so his hero—the master of the game—has to undergo his own abasement of soul—a denial of the value of order and the attractions of young disorder—that unbidden memories of a divided life provide. Meditation (a component of the game) then turns to brooding. However worthy its ideals, it must be admitted that, in actuality, the bead-game cannot be sustained—the remembered uses of power are too insistent. Then chaos resumes: The advocates of the anti-categorical movement (the "Freedom equals License" party) are beating at the gate. Magister Ludi abdicates—citing his own unsuppressed temptations and his weakness at resisting them as evidence of a larger historic failure. He asks his consort Athena (She is the only goddess on Olympus who would tolerate his love of ritual) to flee south with him to a warm place by the sea. But goddesses dislike failures—so she demurs—and returns to the safety of myth. He then asks a boy—a strong swimmer—to accompany him to wherever. They swim together—the ocean is cold—he drowns.

As a consequence, the real degenerates into the actual, and death becomes hollow and static. The end game of recollection—the continuing rearrangement of what can be remembered—the novelty of past history—has no more subscribers. Evidently, then, the past and future of time have both ended. The dependency between the living and the dead, once essential for an after-life, is over.

In Michel Foucault's book "A History of Madness," (2009) an extraordinary practice of theatrical alienation is described. It is a historically factual description, and is first situated in Europe in the latter part of the 15th century—when the practice was most prevalent. Primary references, here, are to a long poem by Sebastian Brand—"Das Narrenschiff "—and to Bosch's famous painting—"A Ship of Fools"—both of that time. The painting has been described as an illustration for the book—but that is not clear. The shared theme, however, is. The poem devotes most of its cantos to a description of aberrations—thus giving an early typology of "deviant" behaviors that were then grouped under the term "fool." (But Brand's descriptions are satirical as well—directed at the authorities sponsoring the "Narrenschiff"). The Bosch painting shows an extraordinary imagistic dialogue of separation and engulfment—between the mad and their created world. The fools are in a small boat—some are in the water—perhaps one is hidden in a tree mysteriously looming overhead. All are playing roles—at but not with each other. One imagines that each would continue to play a role if no one else were there. They all portray various departures from propriety—gluttony, lust, fear, avarice, and the like. The distortions, caricatures, unrealities all point, however, to other worlds—each inhabited only by a single agent—the ascendant, self-sufficient, individual fool. In this theatre of bedlam, there is no contact, no social interchange—only the acting out of private histories and the elaborations of unique obsessions.

The actual practices that are examined in Foucault's book consist of putting a (however) selected group of "deviant" people onto a ship—the so-called "Narrenschiff"—and sailing them from port to port—primarily down the rivers of the Rhineland and into Flanders—where, at each stop, they were exhibited as a theatrical spectacle, a show of deviance—for the amusement, bemusement, or enlightenment of the paying public. There was no script, no rules—the civic leaders who devised the practice evidently considered the antics of the mad to be sufficiently inventive and entertaining (or horrific) not to need a script or direction. The overall social purpose, however, was to provide an example of punitive control that separates the mad from the sane—and so protects the state.

In other periods—e.g., the early middle ages—the spectacle of the fool was regarded more positively—as giving signs of other-worldliness, a disdain for earthly trappings—even a closeness to God. "Fool" did not then have the later connotations of "social deviant"—or the modern connotation of "medically impaired." Rather, for the believers, madness signified a release—into innocence, perhaps into spirituality—an unquestioning acceptance of life's travails, a rejection of conformity, and a direct path to salvation. There were penitent saints a-plenty in the fields and villages to corroborate this image. Later, however, the interpretation changed: Madness and eccentricity came to be seen as a disregard for the penitently

LIFE AND DEATH

spiritual and obediently civic, and thus became a symbol of God's disfavor. Vilification, abuse, and incarceration was the called-for response, and the "Ship of Fools" turned from a theatre into a prison—a place of punishment. Such sequestering was also a good fiscal method for ridding the cities of unwanted indigents. But throughout the course of these practices—both early and late—the role of the insane remained didactic—a lesson for the sane. Early on, the antics of fools were a sign of holiness—a desired insanity. Later, they were turned into evidence of criminality and incipient damnation—the latter feeding the former by providing good reasons for incarceration and punishment. In the present day, "aberrant behavior" has become a symptom of illness—medical or social—and important questions now arise about distinctions between the two. But throughout—however historically situated—the mad are seen as gadflies, and sometime teachers—of the sane.

As communal attitudes continued to evolve, the insane "actors" in the "Ship of Fools" responded to the changes in their reception and their treatment with changes in their own behavior. When exclamations of delight turned into abuse, when food became scarce and brutality became the norm—the (unwritten) script also had to change. The affects of insanity turned into an assault on the conventions and beliefs of the audience. Other performances—more direct or more bizarre- were built upon the contents of insanity—and upon the intensity of its experience for the "fool." Some of these works embraced spontaneity—as with direct acting-out—which anticipates the "immediacy" of action painting. Others were more elaborately contrived foreshadowing the conceptual intricacies of Surrealism, and the political ambitions of Living Theatre. When such "aesthetic" presentations were met with punishment, the response inevitably was that of more extreme behavior—protests, manifestos or criminal activity. From a liberal perspective, the mad are often justified in stretching the others' antagonisms. A sufficient period of degradation would make anyone—even the sanest—act up and protest—and such protests invariably take the most abrasive course. As described by Foucault—such manifestations as public incontinence and nudity, sexual distortion and grotesquery, scatology in speech and body—became the script for now self-scheduled appearances.

Foucault's "History of Madness" evinces a philosophical mix of sense and chaos—of virtual life and immanent death. They (the exhibited subjects) are like us but not like us—they are both human and non-human (inhuman? once-human?). They are neither rational nor anti-rational—but somewhere situated in the great irrational—all of which, in the context of life and death—provide a fecund mix of contending opposites.

I interpret the "fools" as the living-dead. They provide a look across to the other side—a symbolic view of the reality that has no viable currency for the living. But it is there—that reality—a factoid that inhabits descriptions (like mine) of non-being, or post-being. The fools are a harbinger, a warning, a narrow escape—"there but for (fill it in) go I." They also provide a glimpse of the other side—on the assumption—given the poverty of their present—that there is one.

Audience curiosity does not linger long on any spectacle. The sane, although often enjoying the contrast of grotesqueries, well know where they live. The fools, having scratched some skin off genteel curiosity, are then herded back, to be taken to other places where they remain in confrontation with their demons. All places, in fact, have that need, but only some are willing to pay—and so—exhibitions of the insane-degenerate-ecstatic—wagging breasts and dangling testicles, public sex, incontinence-on-call—proclamations of sacrilegious doctrines—they don't come cheap these days.

But think—say the city fathers, of the practical value! The mad-exhibited leave behind memories of their otherness. In short time—don't you know—their twitches will become traffic signs within a municipal code of vehicular creativity; their drooling will offer suggestions for the proper response to the foreign influx of hotly spiced cuisine; their erratic gestures can become a training manual for our expeditionary forces—or used instead as a primer on how to be noticed at parties. Most memorably, though, the mad (disenfranchised, incarcerated, delegitimized) show the fragility of the boundaries between custom and discord, habit and novelty, the agreeable and the unspeakable, past and future—life and death. This is educational. But then there is the contrarian belief: All these aberrations—despite the romantic attraction of open boundaries—clearly show our duty (no?) without malice (yes!) to strengthen (for the sake of our children) the real distinction between us. But how to do this—and remain safe—is a problem. Build more barriers!

As my concern here is with life and death, I take the ship of fools as a guide, an entrance into my pre-occupations with the changing status of being—when it is followed, as fools will do, by the leavings and becoming of memory and anticipation. We, sometime fools, seek—together with the truly mad and incompletely dead—a guide to what our "now" really comes to. This is an important bit of seeking—one that can be (partially) extracted

LIFE AND DEATH

from methods of the ancient prophesies (choose your own) that illuminate the actuality (and inevitable disappearance) of our here and now. This vulnerability helps to underscore the distinction between the actual and the real. I have argued that "reality" is more fragile, yet it is larger, and comes later—if at all—than does "actuality." We may die before we acknowledge the reality that would include the picture of own traverse across actuality. Lacking this insight, we might as well be nothing—just dead.

XX

CONFESSIONS

So what am I—living or dead? Wait—don't go! Who's asking? That's important too—I want to know. The where and when of it will follow on—once you tell me who or what you are.

On face, it should be easy: If I'm talking, I'm alive—if not, I should be dead. But—see—you're reading this, so you wouldn't know without asking some other one (an erstwhile friend or foe) about my where and when. Don't do that yet—know that it's not easy for me either. There is a where and when of writing this—but right now, it's not a now for either you or me. We can't know that now from where we are. Still—I ask you not to ask the others—they (really) don't know anything about our now. Speaking of those others: I'm sure you would rather that I be writing this (directly and only) to you. It was our agreement (no?) together with ongoing love, perpetual sex, the best of local food, and occasional trips to the country.

But I wasn't completely truthful—it's part of my charm, as you once said. I do want lots of people to read this and then talk with others—it doesn't matter what they say. Talking—whether during my lifetime or after—is the real but not always the actual issue. Then too—if time weren't so willfully linear I could add "before" to our talking—which I could then include within the real—but not the actual. Talking in the actual is always "during." Remembering (what you said) comes "before." The real, however, is broader—a lot of it is already there before we talk. That real is as yet mute—and not a part of the actual. (Lovers often face this problem). But we can envision a kind of time that—in other configurations—behaves better than it does now. Then we could talk about all this before I write it. We should all then know—in the after that now is reachable—what it is that I will write—and you will read.

CONFESSIONS

You might think of my writing as a covert performance—a visitation by the latest of the boated mad—a proffered simulacrum of the living and the dead—a play in a when-less where-less there that (despite you) includes both you and me. But one of us has to be alive to do the reading and the writing: You show up and I am there alive—so much to the good. We can then resume the food, sex and, yes, talking—which, between the times of writing, I have sorely missed.

The cast of my play is composed of memories—who and what of our where and when. Not surprisingly, this compendium makes for lots of folks—a big cast—that may become larger still because you haven't told me everything about yourself, nor have I about myself to you. These evasions could be justified by the fact that we've both forgotten a lot—or maybe, that it doesn't really matter—it is only idle chatter.

> But you and I both know the signs of secrecy—
> the sweaty flush, e.g., that shows up before the morning pea,
> and then disappears down the river and into the sea.
> Flushes, nonetheless, must be shown and seen.
> They work to protect a dream from ending early—
> when still unconnected with culpability.

To give our origins due substance, I believe that we should view their world from the vantage of other times and places. Which ones? Why, any and all that we have once been in. We can also fabricate or borrow if need be—that's part of what we've got. Now, think some more about dreaming: Which aspects of the world do we have when we dream—more than one, for sure. In dreams there is a kaleidoscope of fragments that appear, rotate, and vanish uncompleted, as we go our dreamy way. We are not here nor elsewhere in dreams, nor are we now or then. We have no idea what happens next—nor do we know that we should care—until we come awake. Upon awaking, we usually reach—just quickly—back to memories that were present in our dreams. But actually, we remember very few. Dream-memories have no sympathy for our waking past—nor (pace Freud) do they offer solutions for our future—and that is because their revelations do not present problems for our solving when awake. They also offer no recipe for self-betterment. Although dreams may scold at times, they scold the dreamer—but give no hint of what's to come at daybreak. The time of dreaming has no need for waking time. To think of dreams when awake is to ruminate.

Now I ask you: Would you recognize your dreaming self—if you met him wide-awake? Of course not! Who is this creature? Call the cops! You dream yourself in and out of the memories that come unbidden as you dream them. The one that dreams—the "you" in your dreams—is not your waking you. It is the one formed—as is often said—by repression, revelation, fantasy of achievement, fears of abandonment, premonitions of failure—everything, actually. A heavy dinner with ample wine can affect a dream—but so can a forlorn face seen on the midnight train. There are dull dreams as there are dull people—but the two don't resemble each other. If dream diving were as far advanced as is dumpster diving, the spinster living silently across the street would be as richly revealing of her essence as Gibbon was of Rome's. But she won't and you have no access to her dreams—so don't judge, when waking, the revelations in, even, your own dreams.

You can't because the you in dreams is other—in place, time, sequence, identity—than your waking self. But it presents the present subject of dying with a clue: To think of yourself as historically alive or dead could employ a similar strategy of displacement as does dreaming. Aristotle is alive and well in history; Heidegger is doing tolerably well in his smaller span. Aristotle had Aquinas and Hegel to speak for him (to keep him—as it were—alive). Heidegger is an important bulwark for late Existentialism—the doctrine of deep and solitary diving. But (for all of us) there are counter-currents: Aristotle's causal nexus points (through St. Thomas and Hegel) to God's will instantiated in secular progress. This has recently lost him (Aristotle) some attention. Heidegger, for all his smarts, was timid enough to weave the mythic origins of the "master-race" into his concern for a present "authentic being"—and may not recover. But we should give both a later look.

You and I are scattered among the footprints made by people who read or look or otherwise remember. A small terrain—to be sure, but that is where we are. It's all too recent—I may still be alive when you read this—maybe not. But we, as inhabitants of the fickle attention of the "span of memory"—(another way of saying "History")—live in keeping with the varying fortunes of the histories of recollection. Both alive and dead, we are the sum and interplay of ideality and reality—and are thus, dependent on memory.

Notice sadly, that there are many who seem to evade this summing—and so disappear without a trace. That is why the living so adamantly engage in finding lost bodies, performing funeral services, exhibiting sacred bones, embalming, erecting memorials, publishing obituaries. It is an expiating, as I believe, by the concretely living for their prior neglect of those now abstractly dead. It is also a plea for a "decent burial" (whatever that accomplishes) when one ones-self is dead.

So I must ask, then: Do you think that what I write here is a directive for the celebration of my own demise? Not really.

Of course, any celebration that includes me—or, better, is about me—is one I welcome. But I prefer celebrating my living while alive rather than when dead—celebration is more fun in the actual world. Think of it! The old venerable—all gussied up in sandals, loin-cloth and a straw-hat- chowing down on crisp brisket, hot red beans, and salad—lolling in the shallows of a temperate sea—surrounded by fair admirers who are shielded from his (now mostly ceremonial) grasps and lunges by their young intemperate quickness. This is a welcome vignette—however much the disparity in accomplishment between lunge and avoidance casts a painful light on the actuality of age and creaky joints.

But call me—I'll do my best to show up.

XXI

BEYOND POETRY

Beyond—poetry?
Such austerity; verging on pomposity.
But it is nevertheless the case
that poetic truths will get us nowhere
but to where we are—
hunkering between our week-old underwear
and the sweetish smell
of another's tiny oh so lovely toes.

These are truths not available to multitudes.
Good thing.
Toes are fragile—they bear the marks
of how they once were badly used.
Toes are beneath fingers in the ledgers
of necessity.
They will not play a flute or shine my shoes.
But they are requisite for climbing hills
and showing-off in showers.

I like my large and bony toes.
They do just fine when kicking rocks
so as to teach the world it's real.
But I preferentially love the tiny toes
of seemly folk who squeal when touched.

XXII

THE NEW PURGATORY (Preface)

CAN YOU CONCEIVE OF a purgatory without purpose—a place that moves and changes in ways that go nowhere—not a where at least, that has a "there" at its beginning or end? That's what death is like—and, as I sometimes think, life is too. So you see, it's not just nothing—although the something that it is—is not always (pace Wittgenstein) say-able. But we (some of us) are now prone to accepting the unsayable as real—and then to find deviant ways of saying (or showing, or playing) it for others.

    I dislike the received notion of purgatory—because of its origins in sin and expiation. But here, I put my own notion to a different use. The traditional Purgatory (the "way-station" model)) is usually pictured as a spectacle of shorn sheep, eyes downcast, trudging ever upward, and growing new wool as the terror of the lower flames became more remote, and the cold clouds of salvation begin to wrap around and lessen anxieties about the pain of burning. It's a noisy progression—with confessions of guilt and pleas for mercy growing ever louder as the trail gets steeper. Plainsong that was first composed (during the early days of hard-belief) in chants and motets, then takes on the complexities and revelations of counterpoint. As one climbs higher (and belief becomes less critical) the sounds of penitence evolve—first to musicals, and then into rock and rap. The original intricacies of formal demonstration of belief are no longer needed as Heaven looms ahead. The Heavens in turn—pleased with such demonstrations (however) of the continuity of faith—resound: A C-major chord, of course: Welcome pilgrims—to bliss for all eternity! (A question for the living: Are the Bach passions—or Beethoven's Ninth—or Mahler's eighth—ever played in Heaven? But then, given the alternatives—why should they be? Ask the Lord! Another question: If it so happens that Grunewald's Isenheim

Altarpiece, or Michelangelo's Last Judgment could be rescued from earthly oblivion, and displayed on Heaven's walls—would there be curator-saints to place them properly? Where would they be exhibited? What would be said about them? What is Heaven really like?

My purgatory, unlike the one I describe above, needs no Heaven—because it goes nowhere. Oh—there are mountains and valleys, true, but there also are valleys without mountains (although not mountains without valleys—that is the Devils domain). Don't feel deprived, however. There are the ever-tranquil seas, verdant plains, blowing winds from mild to sharp. And there are goodies left from other times—such as succubae and incubi, nectar and ambrosia, and many armed goddesses. We all wash together in sylvan ponds—but no longer desire further immersion with each other. This is not forbidden, but has no point—as there is no present to be penetrated for good reason. (Pre-Christian inhabitants still think otherwise). This Purgatory is in its developmental stage—it is for folks just learning how to read new books. Heaven has already had its adequate descriptions. My new purgatory also has a plethora of dinosaurs, nymphs and satyrs, giant carnivorous ferns, warthogs, and lots of bugs and snakes—sufficient to every taste.

The demarcations of taste, here, are both democratic and programmatically unclear—but as all are equal, the contrasts are offered without argument. These characteristics—equality and vagueness—are essential to my construal of life after death. From all I have said, one might think that my purgatory is a receptacle—like Plato's—the source, repository, and sum of all things past and future. Not far off. I do think of death as a receptacle—something that is always there yet always wanting to be reconsidered, refilled, and so, revitalized. Death is the past immersed—as is the persona of an exotic dancer—within changing interpretations.

Some may say that without an individual consciousness, there are no interpretations to speak of. This may be a truism—but it is indeed difficult to affirm a consciousness without the prefix of "individual." Many have tried: "Cosmic Consciousness," "Collective Consciousness," "Robotic Consciousness," and the like. But these do not do the work proposed—we are not "at one" with anything outside us—we remain the squabbling scheming horde that is human society. But this last conceit—Robotic Consciousness—is interesting—and topical—because it questions the boundaries between humans and the created others—automata. We would (some of us) be delighted (would we not?) to have robots constantly work for us, programmed to

THE NEW PURGATORY (Preface)

"cheerfully" provide for us—but not replace us. If that were to happen, then the gap between automata and people would begin to resemble the one between social and economic classes.. But will our "intelligent" (almost-conscious?) robots face-up to the conundrum of our eventual demise—and their incipient obsolescence? Will they glimpse, across the boundaries, the human difference between "actual" and "real? Or will they, like dogs, watch for us each evening at the station—whether or not we show?

In Stanley Kubrick's film "Space Odyssey," Hal—the computer-brain of the space ship, begins to assert "his" claim to autonomy by tampering with the programmed nature of the flight. In doing so, he violates the categorical separation between "mechanical" and "human"—and comes to understand that his (somehow) emerging capacity for free will is a hope for transcending separate realms of being. In this scenario, humans have played God and have created a machine that, in some critical (but not every) respect, is human—somewhat as God re-created (an aspect of) himself as human. The crew on the space-ship, unnerved by this theological breakdown of absolute categories, enact a latter-day crucifixion—they pull out overreaching Hal's structural components, watch him recede into child-like babble—and then into silence. Not as brutal as Gethsemane—but, mythically, almost as consequential. I think of Hal as a post-biblical transgressor before his time (as was Christ)—but also as a harbinger of the new-realm relationship (human-divine, mechanical-human) necessary for the expansion of life into a higher place of Being.

There may be another receptacle (as in Plato's "Timaeus") that contains everything past and present, and there may be a way of being that is without consciousness—but, thinking more about it, I don't think so. A place that contains "everything" is illogical—there is no "everything" without something outside—even if outside expands into itself—which is then pure inside with a problem. But that, too, seems illogical. Anyway, a place that does not contain "consciousness" is a bad place in which to tell a story. Such places are a modern theologian's nightmare. But the past is full of them—burnt-out worlds, dead civilizations, extinct species, mute people. Apologists don't want to cede to God a universe with nothing that remains of everything He left out. This description—"everything"—as I see it, is a pot of being cooked to overflowing—with nothing to flow into. Make another pot! Call it what you will! Create a parallel universe without (a) god. On all such counts: God is not possible without consciousness.

ISSUES AND FRAGMENTS

I think my "New Purgatory" is like a dream—better, a dream of dreaming. In this way I escape being nothing, and instead, can write on to tell you stories about life and death. These stories—as I tell them—are the wary but essential co-habitants of dreaming. What makes them wary is the fickleness of time—whether or not it ever stops. What is essential to them is me—the author behind the writer who concocts this tale. You see, I am writing in my here and now, quite alive as I believe, and somewhat enjoying the fiction (if that is really what it is) of inhabiting another state of being. However—you my readers, are not singular—as I, in my present place, believe I am. You are various—although (of course) singular within yourselves—but you are not, no one of you, in my time of writing. When you read this, I might well be dead—or, more irritating to you—still alive before you have finished reading and after you yourself have died. (But don't blame your death on me).

The sober point is that you are reading what I'm writing in some other here and now. I am finished when you read it to the end. After completion, like a perfect storm or a completed thought, we go our separate ways—you to mull, and I to find new memories, and write some more.

But how to describe the world we inhabit in the interim—when we are both together—bound by a common time that neither of us, from other viewpoints, is or was or will be in? I suggest that there is a time that is neither "same" nor "other"—a time that has no need of "is-was-will." It is a time of novel repetition, of changing ritual—a multi-dimensional, non-linear time—that does not cater to the needs of fear or aspiration, progress or failure. Death does have such a time—but it is not the same as the time of dying. It has no concern for the can of ashes resting on the mantle.

In my story, the dead travel to the new Purgatory, where they assess the gap between their memories of themselves and the memories others have of them. As this assessment has no practical value ("practicality" having no place in the New Purgatory) it comes closer to the Kantian ideal (in the Third Critique) of "judgment"—which only the dead can fully entertain. This form of judgment is not "determinate," but "reflective."—as its interests are not in explanation, but in contemplation—which, in turn, seeks its subject in the "harmony" between the components of perception. The time of contemplation mimics that of death, for only in such a time—movement without direction, change without cause—can a totality be present. The time of life, in contrast, moves as does the time of explanation—for its subject is always partial.

THE NEW PURGATORY (Preface)

When one living asks: "what does it all mean?"—or "why must I die?"—one answer is to be found in the difference between a language and its reference. What we speak about, and the characteristics by which we presume to know what it is to "speak about"- are systematically elusive. Reference occurs in a different time than does its object. We exercise our rationality to buttress our hope that both are connected—and will give us what we need for living—which it often does. This hope gives us our "present." But non-pragmatically—it is a most elusive giving. We cannot speak of anything "now" that is not "before." The locution "will be" marks a time of anticipation—but what will be may never be. "Was" is our time of (authenticated) reference—but authenticity is subject to choices between competing narratives: "What was it that then happened?" In-between, there is a "now"—but it is nothing we can point to, much less speak of—at the same time: "What is it you now are saying?"

XXIII

QUOD EST DEMONSTRANDUM

THE USE OF LOGIC in the demonstration of how a world is—is for me, less a speedboat than a dugout, or a leaky canoe. But its authority hovers—how else to get from here to there? Try a trip with me: We will go upstream; and if we lose our way, we can float back down to where we once began—or if we capsize, we can swim across to a shore where we have not been.

(x)—What is that? Where did it come from?

x (Fx)—Better. If I understand you right, you say that for any x at all—it is (an) F.

But, to begin our story—that last is problematic: "Any x-at-all" is "every x there is"—and how can we know (about) all the things there are?

Then there is the problem of this (F): It is designated as a value (a specification of the variable x). But how can we know? Is it Sensible? Supersensible? Bi-sensible? Trans-sensible? Non-sensible? Which do we look for? Which do we accept?

Then there is this further problem: Are F's [values] as prolific as—less or more so—than are x's [variables]?

It would seem "more so." Splitting a variable—x—could be considered murder, while splitting (re-designating) an F—value or attribute—would simply be following the dictum—that between any two least discernible—there is something less discernible.

Return to: x (Fx)—The claim is that whatever there is—it must be something—to exist.

But existence in itself [as Kant said} is not a predicate—so any x must be an F (some aspect of existence) in order to exist.

Now: x, ∃y (Fx > Fy)

This is the (opportunistic) claim that there is something that is like everything—namely—it is F.

But: ∃x (~Fx. Gx)

This claim states that if there is something that is not F—then it is G

But: ∃x, ∃y (Fx . ~Gx : Gy . ~Fy)

This claim states that there are [at least] two things that are actual but different.

Further: x,y ((Fx.Gy) > ~ ((Fx.Fy) . (Gx.Gy))

This is the important claim that no two things are the same.

Then (a leap): x ((Fx @ T1) > (~ Fx @ T2))

The important claim that no-thing is the same at different times.

The spoiler, here, is time (T). Consider how we fight against time changing. We are prone (asked) to believe that what we believe is enduring, consistently rational and/or God given—that our laws have sway until (lawfully) revoked—that our love is (should be) everlasting, and our friendships always secure. Some, accepting this vein, might well believe that we will live forever if only we can get everything right and at the same time—and so dispense with the corrosions of adventitious change.

If you, my friend, are still afloat with me, please follow on: "T" intrudes here as part of the Devil's domain. The Devil, it is said, has influence on actual (earthly) change—but not the sort of change that leads to a somewhere Good—like Heaven—or the promised land where "the real is rational"—as exemplified by "selfless love." In contrast, the Devil's notion of change is of an invasive worm eating away at our most cherished notions: "Progress," "the persistence of Good," "the achievability of Completeness," "the continuity of Fact," "the inevitability of Death," "the immortality of the Soul."

The Devil is a powerful opponent. He gives change a special focus: He directs it—as an anti-rational attack—against the Pietistic syndrome of success-failure-renewal, where failure becomes success (despite having failed)

because it remains optimistic about the future—a pre-ordained optimism, one that is "given." The Devil's attack is calculated to strip progress from change, and render change non-directional, and anti-teleological. This last—teleology—a belief in the world's eventual culmination, through time, into (Gods) original purpose—is the principal threat to the diabolical. If the Devil were to have his way—change would be immune to purpose and prophesy. The function of time would then be abstract: "Just one damn thing after another"—free will to be neutralized by indifference.

XXIV

THE NEW PURGATORY (Issues)

We now come to that other shore which, at this point in reading, I have only shown you from a distance. I call it "The New Purgatory."

I know it's there—because I believe that nothing ever ends—and that is because "ending" is a matter of transformation, rather than of simple change. Both transformational change and simple change occur between states (states of affairs, states of mind, etc.) Transformations, however, are value-laden—they have meaning (actual and anticipated) for both sides. Simple change is a movement from one thing to another—basically incoherent, yet consequent for action that, itself, is incoherent.

Sometimes, simple change may be mistaken for beginning or ending. This is true in the actual world—where life and empires begin and end—often for no good reason. But it is not true of the real world—which includes dreams, memories, fears and desires, past histories and anticipations of the future—stories about all this, along with the actualities that generate these.

The logical interventions I use above are intended to reinterpret such issues as identity and time in the ways we speak about death and after-death. This move into the exotic could help us focus on the issue of continued identity after (the end of) physical existence, and the nature of that change. One difficulty is the habit of describing past and future in the same sense we apply to present being—where we seek to avoid continuity between the noises of being and the silence of non-being. We make such distinctions as: "The past and future are not the present."—"Being alive is not being dead." These are so true they are better not said—they offer the shelter to rationality of non-contradiction. But logical contradiction entails a term and its negation: $\sim(x \ . \ \sim x)$. But it is the application that matters: "Past, present, future," "alive, dead," are all terms subject to further interpretation before they can be said to contradict each other. The interpretations I offer here do not point to contradiction; rather, they seek transformations that would be true of the transitional relationships between such terms as they (together) occur in consciousness. These are admittedly loaded terms; they carry a modicum of uncertainty and dread because they refer to states of being that are us—but occur beyond the limits of our actuality.

The contrast I use above—between "being" and "non-being" is somewhat harsh—as one member evokes everything there is—and the other a notion-less (non-consciousness) state of nullity—a world without perceivers. But I use the term as a goad in my efforts at accounting for the transformation of "being" into what can be called a "Mulligan-stew:" anything and everything goes into the pot. But because (at this reading) we are all laden with sequential being, we can only (in defense) locate the term "post-being" in the realm of speculative metaphysics—as in existential attempts at coping with non-being: e.g., "To not be is worse than to minimally be." (There is always hope). Or—"To will not ever having been is worst of all." (There is no such thing as hope). The impact of linguistic change in all this is indicated by the location of "being" in both past and future—moving as a straight line through the present. Our conception of human identity as occurring within a progressive history evokes the theory of a human exceptionalism within nature: "Only humans have a soul." My conception of extending identity into realms of "post-being" is a philosophical gambit—a fanciful journey, a trip of the imagination—to an alternative (post-actual) reality which I call the "New Purgatory"—in which the bad manners and the bloody predilections of the still alive and linearly historical, are rinsed—not discarded—but come to merge with others of a different flavor, and within a finer stew.

XXV

THE NEW PURGATORY (fragments)

My model is of a game that is not a game—for it is not one for winning. In this sense, it is somewhat like Wittgenstein's account of language as a game—an unending and overlapping series of linguistic constructs through which people in different places and times, while not governed by any single set of rules, are yet connected by "family resemblances." There are equally many directives in my New Purgatory—all tell everyone what can be done—but there are no rules, no stipulations as to which relationship fits a circumstance and which does not—for that would be inhibitive to immortality. But there is much source-material available—there is all of history, everything that has been lived, and all that can be imagined. To achieve completeness is an ideal—but that's the way it is over here. We have the post-temporal leisure for the consummation of ideals. As with languages, a speaker is required. When language is ritualized into a game, a master—who is sufficiently erudite, and institutionally capable—directs the play. (I resurrect "Magister Ludi"). Also required are traditions sufficiently "rule-like" to elicit and further family resemblances—for players in eternity must remain aware of each other. The languages that are in play expand and diminish as these traditions change through the materials they have access to—depending not only on history, but on the contributions of the living and the to-be living. It follows that no language is fully understood (even by its speaker) and no language completely disappears—for it once was used, then changed, and later in some part remembered.

  The New Purgatory is modeled on language in the sense that it is structured by its use. (No use is useless here). The components of this usage are memories and dreams—recollections and reconstructions of events, once actual now historical—all now equally fictional—that are the sum of all that has transpired in human consciousness. As I hold "consciousness" to first be individual and then collective, its amalgam into the reality of New Purgatory is an additive process—each player and baggage auguring a new game—which, in turn, requires a reconfiguration of an older game. This process replaces time—as it does not generate novel events, but remakes those that have been offered as history (and all those that will be offered to history). This remaking, I consider to be a "schematic reconfiguration" of the given—change that is independent of physical time. In this sense, it can be called "new." It is the New-Purgatory alternative to the earthly notions of "time passing." As there cannot be a comprehensive set of memories—recollection of the past never being complete—all events in the world of living, once lived—become part of the syntax available for the games of post-life. The nature (procedure) of each game—its semantics and its uniqueness—depends on the interactions of its players—the expanding society of the dead. There can be heroic interchanges—Akhenaton talks with Marx—Venus with the Virgin Mary—Brooklyn Lucian with Roman Lucian. But most interactions (like most players) are modest—which does not speak against their richness: Every game, stylistically, is fully realized. These qualities—of plenty and its broadest expressions—replace the qualities of particular truths and parsimony that are too often found in earthly games. Here—more is more. The New-Purgatory aesthetic is formalistic in procedure—but expressionistic in its body.

There are a lot of dead here—more so than are living. But they are not all players. (As on earth, we have our malcontents). Numbers of applicants and kinds of backgrounds change as recollections and anticipations of the still living expand or contract in accordance with the contributions of past and future. Well—that's nice to say—but (really) who are they—from among all those that we (now dead and in principle free of earthly prejudice) will accept as players for the games in Purgatory? Are all such players limited to dead humans—– or can anything once alive become a player? That is a sore point—even here. Whether animals (or even plants) can be players in the game (as bona-fide members of the New Purgatory) remains controversial in Cosmological politics. Some of the conservative adherents to a dualistic theory of creation—say "no"—for they insist that plants and animals are lesser beings without a soul. And being without a soul, they say—what plants and animals did when alive was neither right or wrong—it just was. Where then—if we let them in—would be the measure of "just-desserts"—which still applies to us? Further, they argue, there

THE NEW PURGATORY (FRAGMENTS)

were no plants or animals in the Old Purgatory. Those folks, beleaguered as they were by later doctrine, knew enough to follow the old differences between people and everything else. The cosmic radicals, lately in ascendance, counter (as they once did on earth) by emphasizing "equality." They hold that these other species, just like us, were once alive—and, given the new sense of creation—they have the same rights. Cautious centrists (a declining number not willing to risk losing a wager on the ways of eternity) say "a limited (chosen) few can play." They warn, however, that these lesser creatures are like the pawns in chess—they move slowly, but they'll take you down if you let them get to the left or right of you—and eventually, as we know, some pawn (not all, of course) can become a queen. Then where, even dead, will we be?

The Master of the Game, himself undemocratically chosen, has an eternity appointment to adjudicate such questions. But there is no rush, as there is no sequential time for wasting—there are only games to play. And, as there is no winning—all disagreements just result in other games. (I suspect that the conservative dead, unhappy with such equanimity, will petition to return to the Old Purgatory). But recollection in the New Purgatory is bottomless, rich, and open—whales converse with willow trees, soldier ants with major generals, Lao Tzu with Mao. Both syntax and semantics in the gaming become more sophisticated with each passing play.

> No- one here is ever bored—they say,
> but
> no-one gets—his or hers or its—own way.

You might well ask how this realm of the New Purgatory relates to the other realities—of Heaven and Hell—to the Old Purgatory—and indeed, to that source of its ongoing possibility—the actual world.

The long-established institutions—Heaven and Hell—have long had their share of trouble. For one, they are not yet clear about the nature of temporality—some aspects of which they insist on sharing with actuality, others with reality. As we remember: Heaven has had two revolutions—the occurrence of Evil (Satan's fall), and the Creation of the World (temptation and sin). Each revolution seems a necessary condition for the other: We cannot easily hold, e.g., that Heaven "always" contained evil; or that the Devil was evil "from the start;" or that God did not, "at every point" know (etc.) all of what was going on. But then, these difficulties suggest that Heaven has been given a temporal aspect (by us) for its eternity. We should have a better model. Humans seem always to require a "before and after" to explain their difficulties. But even if we suppose that the notions of time and fate are not linked, we should want the transition in Heaven—from before to after the first occurrence of evil (Satan's fall)—to correlate with the before and after of the expulsion of Adam and Eve from Paradise (evil's second occurrence) and to the consequent becoming (inter—alia) of you and me.

The ensuing conflict, however theologically parsed, between good and evil—and its resolution via the agency (and vicissitudes) of contingent mortals—is often pictured by the traditional paths that await the further journeys of the after-dead. These traditionally are: The Pains of Hell; Heavenly Bliss; and the penitential journey (the old Purgatory) to avoid the one and attain the other. The relevant images are everlasting pain, eternal bliss, and sequential expiation. The Last Judgment marks the end of (earthly) time as sequence—for Heaven does not contain time: Eternal Bliss, however pleasurable and forever, is static. Hell-fire (numbingly) is also static. But expiation is another matter—as it is in the middle, it must move.

I am interested in the infirmities (linguistic—or if it so be—actual) of the Old Purgatory. I begin by citing two degenerative symptoms: The continuing obsession with time, and the rote need for expiation. Time is a necessary factor in the Old Purgatory, for it measures the rate of penitence that sinners must show as they trudge upwards toward their goal of eternal bliss. This is not modeled on the one-time smart-show of repentance, common in earthly courts—that is calculated to produce a lighter sentence. In the realm of after-death—as St. Augustine says—there are no secrets, no guile. God is omniscient. Secrets and elicited confessions belong to the politics of absolute monarchies and earthly dictatorships—and (should) have nothing to do with the protocols of after-death. So the worst of us—malefactors that are known by their vile behaviors (and secret beliefs)—are punished forever in the flames of Hell. The lesser sinners—those weasels of circumspect evil—are given the opportunity of repentance by their dumb show throughout the purgatorial ascent. This is more civilized than the ordeal of fire—more in keeping with the recent legal sentence of "pen-indef" (penitentiary indefinite)—where exemplary behavior behind bars gets you out faster.

In the New Purgatory, however, the changes in doctrine are sufficiently critical (in both the programmatic and the aesthetic sense) to be considered both new, and critical. But these changes are not leveled at the

THE NEW PURGATORY (FRAGMENTS)

temporal sequences of life-death-judgment. Rather, their context includes the lives of the historically living, and the variations that comprise the occasion of having lived. This amalgam requires restraint, equanimity, tranquility—and constant revising. It also is specific to the nature of the game. The dead, bereft as they are of bodily juices and earthly desires, have (through that loss) gained the requirements for playing the New-Purgatorial game.

But this is indeed a peculiar state of being—game-play without juice or desire? No chance of winning? Nothing left to win? How and why go on? Good questions! So the status of the dead—their singular reality as entities—needs further discussion.

The life of the dead is not a continuation of actual life—for then, actual death would only be a bag of bones, a tin of ashes, or perhaps—more dramatically—some shark or tiger shit. A Resurrection would be required. We the living, in contrast, are discrete and self-protective as physical beings—but are less confined as mental entities. Alive, we assuredly grow older—unless we trade our actuality for our representations—as did Dorian Grey—but then we must face the perdition of becoming our representations—which are often made by inferior artists. As mental entities, however, our early ambitions to excel at running or wooing, give way—as we grow older—to the less physically centered ones of understanding, recapitulating—perhaps finding peace through changes in self-placement within all we have come to know. Well, maybe not all—but some goodly part—if we are honest with ourselves.

The diffusion of the self into the holistic understanding is much like Spinoza's definition of the soul—the "I" as merging with the "All." It is also an apt description for the players of the bead-game, where time as progress gives way to time as recapitulation. Its endurance as an image describes the game itself—in the sense that an inclusive pantheism does not want conceptual or social boundaries. But the largesse of this diffusion makes it a better model for New Purgatory than for our world. Players of the N.P. game watch changes in the vicissitudes of their world much as children watch changes in a kaleidoscope. Each image is complete—no two are ever alike. All images are perfect in themselves, but none is better than another. The players themselves are now compendia of their lives—beyond praise or blame—sufficient (but unnecessary) for the games continuation. There are always players with nothing more to add—truths about ones-self are soon forgotten. This is a danger—for some may have been so unformed in life as to not be—even in the New Purgatory—one that can play the game.

But the partialities of forgetting and remembering are only a formal safeguard—there is no "completeness" to either—so "non-being" (emptiness) is here, at worst, an extended exile: "Go into the desert, sit on a rock, and try to remember." The specifics of memory define the parameters and participants of each game—and they recast the rules as new additions render them inadequate or parochial. These uncertainties insure the continuity between games. They also ensure the afterlife of the players.

Foucault's "History of Madness" (as I discuss above) gives us various narratives that can be of use at this point: In the Bosch painting "Ship of Fools," the characters are types—standing for the vices and virtues, dispositions and oppressions, of socially deviant humans. Each is a slice of history that continues beyond individual existence. The fools have lived their lives and now exemplify it—much as do the dead. Being complete in themselves (whether crazy or dead) they do not need each other—although their groupings tell the larger story of how it can be to live in alienation. The ship, as pictured, is a floating gourd—it could go any which way, or it can spin in place. The inhabitants look all ways, in and out of memories, but not ahead—for that is the direction of the sane. One cannot know from the resident fools, which way the ship is going. Perhaps the ship, like the expanding universe, continues to go while going nowhere. There is infinite time in which to go nowhere—but it is not a comfortable time for the living-sane.

The Brand book that I note—"Das Narrenschiff"—tells the story of a historical voyage that begins with entertainment and amusement, degenerates into sickness and sadism, continues on to indifference and incarceration—and, later, adopts the values of diagnosis and palliation. This can be taken as a parable of actual life. The fools know this (as fools will do) and so they respond by becoming their own improved story. They move from actual to virtual life by acting other than who they are. This "once removed" is a measure of protection from actuality and a prescient move into reality. The suffering is in taking—as themselves—their masquerades. It is their "Via Dolorosa."

XXVI

AT ONE REMOVE

Yes, my darlings—we will recognize each other when once there.
But don't expect the same old chatter.
We can talk of food—Escoffier is around somewhere to help
de-confuse a Daube from an Irish-Stew.
And if we feel too shabby, there are tailors to the King or Queen
who will make us seem more elegant than ever when alive.

As befitting predilections—I will enlist to fight in the greatest battles:
Thermopoly, Gallippoli,
Khartoum, Tarawa, Flanders, and the Bulge.
Waterloo, too—
to name a few.

Upon return—I will cavort with the best that art and dying have to offer:
Too many to mention without danger—to me from you—
when in the judgmental portals of the Nouvelle Vieux.
But here are a few: Venus over Aphrodite—Marilyn underneath Sophia—
Brigitte and Marlene speak in tongues—as we also do.
Memory surely is the thing—to feed the post-life need for consolation
of such as me and you.

XXVII

HOW IT IS THERE

The ritual of game-playing has no limits. The time is never up—the tables are never closed. The account, whether current or long overdrawn, is always being settled by others you may not ever- never know.

There is no Vigorish to pay—so there's only play. But do I have to—always have to—pay to play?

No Sir, not all Sir. We here are infinitely accommodating—but will do nothing else for you—even if you ask us to. It's not like that here—what with the present administration. So you see, Sir—that here, there's no doing for the asking—there's only playing and remembering. Replacing that "asking-doing" stuff with memory gives us all a different power. Dead-people-power is the true equalizer—and the best of enablers too. All races and religions, you see—are free to do what's right (for them) to do.

Whoa! That stops me: "What, after all, is "right," after the living days are done ?" That's a tough one—both for you and me. And that's because one of us (at least) is still alive—which (for both of us—although in different ways) limits understanding of the extended, seemingly inaccessible, parable of right and wrong—i.e.—how "free" fits in with "right."

For starters—try it this way: All of what makes for happy and is good and true—is right (to do). No exceptions: No quibbling about the lurking of fleshly pleasure in "happy," or the social relativity of "good," or the theoretic obscurity of "true," or the practical duplicity of "free." These are earthly problems; they have no purchase here. What is "right" here, is simply a contemplation of the union of desire and memory. In our New Purgatory, the absence of past desire and the richness of present memory complete each other—although some not yet here would say they confront each other! So you see, there is no lack of argument in the New Purgatory

HOW IT IS THERE

—Sacra Conversazione, yes—obscene input, for sure—disbelief, of course—truth, hopefully—conclusion, no-never. This gives our particular take on eternity a patina of variety. Here, when you do what you want to do—it's all right, alright. Yes, you are free—although, once here, you are not free to never having been here—that wouldn't be right. But we'll work it out. You won't be missing anything if you take a walk, or sit still on the ground, or hunker in with others behind the small but everlasting shed—the games don't stop.

The landscape here is as varied as are its histories of bounty, drought, cataclysm, renewal, fire and flood. You have wandered some and looked—now be aware of others—they're all here. Some are prone to change—even as regards their former personae: Enduring mountains and receptive valleys; tyrants or saints; a Madonna or man-killer; behemoths or lowly bugs. Reality, here, is recast through the revisions that the post-dead impose upon received history. What you come in with will change—and change again. But you have the same say as all the others in the changing.

XXVIII

A GARDEN OF FLOWERS

To help smooth the way, I offer some similes—vignettes of places where I've wandered and others that I've only heard about. You can use them as examples of those of yours that you might choose. Mine, actually, aren't much. I've led a sheltered life—except when early in the cities where I used to run around a lot. But my best memories are of the country—I don't know why the New Purgatory is fashioned to be more like country than city. It seems right, though—non-polluted air, open spaces, few prickly pears (but some do mate with poison-ivy so as to astonish the terminally adventurous). No passports, bandits or police—unless you want them for theatrical reasons. The same holds true for Lions and Tigers and Bears.

I once took a ferry from Whidby Island, across the San-Juan straits to Victoria Island. It's a pretty place, more English than is most of Canada. The prettiest parts are their public gardens, carefully planned to sooth the Victorian palette's penchant for uplifting shapes and colors. Oh, a profusion of delights—roses of all shapes and colors, flowers upon flowers, yards and yards of blooming whose names (you'll forgive me) I don't remember. The people are delightful too—well-dressed and mannered—impeccable admirers of the harmlessness of beauty—happily strolling amid the bounties that a well-ordered society can bring.

But I became depressed—(as you would expect, having read this far). It was all too pretty, oh so pretty, much too pretty by far. I hate pretty—pretty can be shitty. So what to do? Nothing. I do nothing in such circumstances—except to imagine what I would do if I were other—more callous, more ferocious, more accomplished, more critical—than I am.

Snakes. That's the answer—the prettiest and most venomous—to blend in and slither through the flowers, waiting for a smiling sniffer to lower a face towards the waiting thorn of fangs. My inventory would start with coral snakes—transverse stripes of yellow black and red to allay the fears of mouse and matron. Then I would introduce the cobras—more for shape than color—their hoods extending as they strike towards the formal smiles of appreciation. Also, Mambas, both black and green—included so as to diversify the latent perils of foliage. And for connoisseurs of pattern and passion, there is the diamond-back rattlesnake. (No constrictors, however—they are too large and have gross eating habits). For ornamental purposes, I would include a scattering of smaller deadlies—such as the Beaded Lizard and the Gila-monster. The first is more attractive than the second. To be bitten, you have to reach out to them—but not to worry—neither will kill a young and healthy full-grown male. As a final bit of sprinkle, I offer some wayward insects—The black-widow spider (females only) for its splash of red—one bite and you're out. And certainly we need the brown-recluse with its violin imprint to necrotize the graphic minded.

The flower gardens, so re-appointed, would then become the symbol of a sterner reality—the collusion of La Belle and Le Betre—the intersection of good and evil—pain and pleasure—eros and thanatos. Good theatre—but more than the city fathers had envisioned.

XXIX

MY SHARK—MY LOVE

Here is another story: I once was a candidate for shark-food—but the tableau unfolded in slow motion, a fairy tale shown at a lesser speed than time ordinarily takes. It was many years ago—fifty years or so—and I was in the Bahamas, seeking a last soul-kiss with the ocean before heading inland to the mid-west to begin another life. But those aspects are not important for this particular story. The part that is—is my meeting with—I tell you—the most beautiful shark.

The story goes like this: After a day of diving, I thought to take a last solitary swim to look at the reef formations and the many-colored fish that inhabit them. This time I swam with only mask, snorkel, and flippers—and as I approached the reef, I saw a shark swimming slowly parallel to—but on the other side of—the reef. O Divina—ma molto periculosa! Her body had an elegance no Venus could match—it seemed so then, although I have never seen a Venus in motion. Then she turned, flipped over the reef, and swam slowly—oh so slowly—toward me. The elegant lines of her tail receded behind a frontal curve whose near point was a Baroque head coming straight out of the recesses of the picture plane. At that point I no longer saw her body—only the expressionless face—eyes set far apart and the large curved mouth, slightly open—the better to show the rows of teeth. Just for you my dear! At that point, I thought that maybe the "she" was actually a "he"—but then I realized that in the transaction between sharks and humans, it doesn't really matter. My shark came within a foot of me, and I could think of nothing to do but turn on my back, put my now thrashing flippers in its face, and contort myself so that I could watch the expanding episode of my potential dying through my faceplate.

MY SHARK—MY LOVE

It didn't take long—a millennium or a minute—and then she turned and—zip—disappeared back over the reef—much faster than when she came. Yes—my she-the-shark abruptly left me. Upon the leaving, I became convinced that it really was a she—who, despite biology, had fallen in love with me—and there-upon had decided not to eat me. I was grateful, true—but I will forever miss her.

I think now of all the mortals taken down beneath the waters to live with mermaids in Neptune's castle—those were the good old days. But actuality, when given a chance, has a way of confounding the pleasures of reality. She—my love—being after-all a shark—should have eaten me. Why she didn't I'll never know—unless she thought it would be better—for both of us—to have me write this story rather than have us disappear into memory—me as shark-shit—and she as only a shark.

XXX

SINGING FOR SPAGHETTI

Here is my last offering—for now—to the memory games of the New Purgatory: I am prone to wandering where no-one goes—where it is dangerous, opaque, unheralded, unseemly—yet intriguing. Some of these places look good right away—others must be stayed with, played up to, before they reveal the beauty of their inner tenants. This form of travelling shows a contrarian impulse of mine—to go to where no one knows me, cannot catch me—and if they do, find they aren't interested in me—at least, not in what I think or do. But there is freedom in these distant lands—a wave of hand—some "howdy" stuff—a few beers—friends forever with no sweat. I used to do that in the eastern city were I come from—back when the desolate drunks, the greenhorn ethnics, and the artist-hopefuls shared porous boundaries. Every one there was wanting—so the boundaries were open to all who tried to know what life—perhaps a made-up life—would be like in places they pass through. But "passing" isn't easy.

    I remember a time in those early years when I was questioned about my presence in a foreign place. It was on Mulberry Street, halfway between Greenwich Village and Chinatown. This was an afternoon in late summer, and I had been wandering around downtown for no remembered reason. I soon became hungry and started looking for a place to eat. But I wanted a special place—where only locals go—no atmosphere or suburbanites. I wanted authenticity—a joining with the unreal people whose lives I knew nothing about—but who, through their own dark powers, did the extraordinary things I had read about.

    I found a small restaurant—without even a sign to identify it. But it seemed reasonably full and bustling—so I went in. I was seated at a small table, alone, which seemed odd, because all the other tables were full. A

SINGING FOR SPAGHETTI

waiter appeared, set down a glass of water, and took my order for meatballs and spaghetti. After a while, a man came by—a large man in a suit. "Live around here?" "Well, yes and no—I live in Brooklyn with my aunt and uncle. I'm a student at Brooklyn College." (I wanted to get it all out at once). "But I also share a place with friends on the Bowery—it's closer to my voice teacher. You see—I think I want to be an opera singer—especially Italian opera—and I'm here to listen to the real melody of the language. I also love Italian food."

This last was true—the former not quite. I was studying voice because of the enthusiasms of my (Italian) high-school music teacher. He was amazed ay my cross-cultural shifts, easy pronunciation, and enthusiasm. But my voice—although pleasant and occasionally mellifluous—was small. My loudest sounds wouldn't fill the far reaches of an auditorium—much less the Met. I remember listening a lot to scratchy record of the greats—Ruffo, DeLuca, Gobbi, Warren—and I would sometimes think: Try to sing like that—but I couldn't do what they could do.

The large man in the restaurant studied me for a while, then said: "Sing an Italian song." No way out—life or death. I stood up, tipping over my chair—and I sang: "Sul Mare Lucicca, L'Astro d'Argento, Placida e Londa" . . . and on and on. I had to sing a lot that afternoon—baritone and tenor arias, folk songs too—no piano—the key didn't matter. But in-between my songs I was fed the best meat-balls and spaghetti, the most fragrant of Chiantis, the most succulent calzone—this side of Mama Lucia's Sicilian Trattoria. My friends for the evening—those huge dark-suited men—tolerated my mispronunciations, memory lapses, and the occasional cracked high note. I received much hand clapping and many bravos. There also were women at the tables– perfumed and heavily made up—early for the hour. They applauded too—although they looked at me somewhat distantly—as if I were a fragile antipasto—a tasty sliver of prosciutto—but not a real meal. After a while (I was growing hoarse and suppressing flatulence) their attention began to wane. Tables emptied, the big men and their companions left quietly—issues of importance needing attention. Cleanup started abruptly, with un-musical clatter—my table was stripped, my ego trampled, and the waiter showed no sign of extending further welcome. So I left—my dream did not follow into the street.

I also like to wander in the country—the pleasure is not only in the walking, it's in the prior selection of gear. I have a large fetish for gear—boots, backpacks, ponchos, camping-tools, gore-tex jacket, heavy woolen sweaters. Over the years, I have accumulated a lot of gear. Before I go, I lay all the items out—as with a sumptuous meal—and the choices I make are the beginning chords of a wilderness fantasy: I inspect them carefully, looking for signs of rust on metal, or dryness and cracking on leather and wood. I protect my gear from such malefactions: Saddle soap on the leather; Linseed oil (boiled not raw) on the wood; Honing oil coupled with a fine stone for the knife. Intimacy and patience—mutual respect—are needed for the process.

But, I do admit, this gives rise to a paradox. I also admire ancient farm implements rusting quietly in abandoned barns—good now only for the looking. Consider the pocket knife, fallen unseen from an overalls pocket many years ago—beyond use now, its time as tool is done, its cutting ended. It lies quietly in my hand, it will not open—it is all corrosion, rust, and pitting—but through its demise as active knife, it maintains a hidden story: wood once whittled, splinters cut out, cans and bottles opened, intruders cowed. Then there is the tire in the ditch—long blown-out, rolled into a gully off the road-edge—where, hidden by weeds and bushes, it has escaped the fate of shredding. Many miles once spent beneath the truck, distant places reached, tales of snow and rain to tell—clearly, a welcome contributor to the games. Perhaps such vulnerable ones—although never having been alive—are a proper part of the New Purgatory—along with those that are more like us. The younger of their kind—the ones still active—have too much ambition to be content with a later life of slow rusting or quiet decay. They want to stay in sight: Houses with large facades, bright sharp knives, deep-tread tires with warrantees—are all the fashion now.

But this infatuation with the new—and programmatically disposable—is, after all, itself a fashion. And all fashions, despite their reputations, are welcome here in Purgatory. Both new and old have their virtues and vices to contribute to the playing. Thinking back: There was once a primeval sameness to which we all are traceable. It was there before the prospect of differentiation became interesting as an activity of existence. Perhaps the differences that are living create the need for after-life summations. And these are never finished as long as life continues.

XXXI

REQUIEM

Don't stir the ashes—the embers are now grey—the fire's gone.
But the smoke still remains, tracing memories of an early brightness.
Moving shapes and shadows, tinkled voices and the soundings of fine glass.
We sat around the fire on a winter's time in deep New Hampshire.
drinking Rum and Raspberries topped with Maple Syrup.
This latter had been carefully boiled,
the scum skimmed off its top until it
reached the pale amber that my companions
look for when they want some extra sweetening.

I came there in a sailor suit—looking for a mooring and recoupling.
For I had been long gone—a life's-time so they said.
And I needed the memories I could still remember—
of all the other ones once gone but still remaining.
They are in the smoke of other memories—
the ones that made my life into the time it had.

Some were still there, drinking rum and berries—as is fitting.
Not much changed, although my eyes are dimmer now.
But the ones I saw, I know, are the realest of the dead—
components of a memory that would disfigure me
were they not still there.

There was uncle Frank and aunt Maria and Tosha too.
Mom and Pop and Marilyn.
Many cousins—first through fourth—some bedecked with progeny:

ISSUES AND FRAGMENTS

Flo and Ray and George with Laura, and Leona—the one I lusted after.

Circumspection remains between my family and anointed friends.
Not surprising—as each looks down a different shape of nose.
But after song and dance, a little talk, and lots of rum—
all agree that, now together (the party was my idea)
we would all be lesser if some left to look for other games.
So they stayed, and acknowledged me as instigator (if not master)
of the present game (it's a complicated story)—
that I am still fashioning for them.

Of remembered friends, I invite only those who are dead—
For, if alive, they would want—as friends will do—
to change the rules of my game.
And although I'm not sure (in writing this)
whether I'm alive or dead—that change I will not do.

Despite vacillations and petty grudges,
my not forgetting dead ones is key to their inclusion:
Ad and Harry, Diller and Jose brought me to my art.
Dick, Bill, and Steven diverted me to philosophy.
(I'm not sorry for this change).
My muses and detractors (legion) are not invited here.
But I might meet them at another party—
and play a different game.

But—
On the supposition that I'm still alive,
I celebrate the living who are my reason:
Samantha, Zoe, Ute.

That will do for me and you.
There's no more for it now.

XXXII

GOD

As is the custom, I end with God.

It is easier to speak of God as cause and center of the universe that to speak of God as source and arbiter of human kind. The universe seems to be going along its way without our help, while here on earth we continue to act abysmally (that is—humanly) despite (or lacking) God's help.

You may notice that I have the devil of a time with pronouns when referring to God. To call God "He" or "Him" is not only an anthropomorphism—but sexist as well. The phrase "God the father" is a political alternative and counter to "Pharaoh" (who themselves were often considered God)—or to "Caesar" (some of whom wanted to be God). There also were female "Gods"—mostly in the ancient East. (Read Graves's "White Goddess"). The Greeks spawned many Goddesses, to the anxious delight of humans (particularly painters)—but old man Zeus reigned over all, although through the ages he seldom acts his age. I would think we're finished with all that. To call God "He" (or "She") is an insult to both women and men—and, to my mind, it also is a theological atavism. (But I believe that it's a social problem as well). I use the term God as direct reference, and "God" as literary reference. I have no problem with the capital "G." But occasionally a small-case god slips in as part of popular usage: "For god's sake!"

To return: It is difficult for me to talk about God because I don't know what (the reference, that is) I'm talking about.

But that is true of other speakers. The subject (God) is usually modeled after what exists—only bigger and better. The lack, or the despairing of a palpable subject—is sometimes marked by shrugs (or a dismissive wave) or silence (broken by intricate analysis of why there is nothing to say)—or a solemn glare leveled prior to your execution. Some say that God is not a real subject—only part of secondary trappings such as Heaven, Hell, Good and Evil, The Real, Eternity and Death—such as are imposed on thought by the need for wholeness and continuity, whether actual or eventual. All this longing then, is to be taken as evidence of a Divine Presence. But some versions of God can also be pluralistic (polytheistic): The gods to be so derived can be as many and various as are the different needs that want satisfaction. The early Greeks were good at this (just look at their Olympic panoply). And even austere Christianity is described by some as polytheistic, with the triune God (father, son, and holy-ghost) having different roles in the divine plan.

But pluralism can be destructive to Dominus—when certain human attributes: grace, civility, authority—usurp the place of the single entity they once were attributes of. This can be a welcome shift in cases where existential fervor replaces ceremonial dogma. For one such as Kierkegaard, however—despite all fragmentations of the human soul—a prior belief in a single God must continue intact. In his "Philosophical Fragments" Kierkegaard examines innate knowledge by reference to Plato's "Meno." In this dialogue, Plato offers the parable of "learning as recollection" as an examination of the question "how we can know without being taught." Socrates, by asking the slave-boy (who is unschooled) a number of connected questions, demonstrates that the boy comes to understand a geometric proof through accessing knowledge that is innate—already in his mind. However this may be, Kierkegaard uses it to support his thesis of "Criterion-less knowledge"—a knowing that does not depend on reference to external sources or to prior axioms for its validity. Here, Kierkegaard shows the extremity—also the intimacy—of his wanted alliance between individual and God. If one has (unexamined) criteria for what one believes one knows, then the choice of belief is not one's own. (It is a "given"). Further, if one refers to specified (theo-logical) criteria to justify belief as prior to one's first examination of belief, then we are two times removed from the self—and, so, from authentic (existential) belief. The choice in that case, to believe in God comes before its reasons. The belief is "unconditioned." This flies in the face of the criteria for scientific belief. "I believe without criteria"- suggests something close to an identity relationship between self and Deity. It is like saying "I believe in myself"—with the hope that the unwanted splitting of "I" from "Me"—thwarted by its felt (and so affirmed) illogic—will corroborate the wanted unity of "I-Myself"—and God.

GOD

But the "I and God"—for most believer—remains separate. So—if one says "I believe in (or on) God" or "I believe that God . . . " the presence of a subject-object connective: "in," "on," or "that" (or some other) mediates the relationship by showing its particular form of distinction. This, I feel, amounts to the interjection, through the connective, of a criterion outside of belief that is for belief. Even if one states the contrary, e.g., "I do not believe in God"—this is tantamount to saying "There—(where?)—is no God." In such cases, one does not achieve transparency between the believer and the object of belief—the reason for agreement or disagreement remains hidden—(elsewhere). Alternatively, one could say "I am God"—this is certainly transparent. But, of course, it will not do at all—for it is an evident lunacy or a power play—a taking for the self, against all common sense, of divine attributes. Another way would be to fudge the direction of reference, and state: "I believe God." This does indicate a fusion—a joining between self and Deity. No aggression here. But the statement put the weight of first utterance onto God, for the implication is that God said something that I believe—much as the statement "I believe in God" puts the weight of credibility onto me.

So I suggest the following: "I believe God \ God believes me." This is dyadic—and so suggests equivalence. It can be expressed by the bi-conditional: I believe in God if-and-only-if God believes in me. We both, God and I, have to make the effort. But even in this form, there is a priority. The first position, in fact, is "I"—even though the implication goes both ways. The linear sequence of language makes such a prioritization unavoidable. But it also may expose a different problem—perhaps also unavoidable. Any utterance about God comes from the speaker. Unless we accept the mysticism of "hearing voices," the speaker is a human person. So, as far as linguistic (if not epistemic) priority is concerned, the "I" comes first. God, historically, has often been asked to answer.

But the appeal to equivalence can also be an appeal for acknowledgement of a union, without subservience or domination—between the self and God. Perhaps this is what Kierkegaard had in mind. There is no slave, no vassal, no servant, no subject—no lord and master. There is (should be) only a striving for a true union—which will then give its reasons to its parts.

But what sort of union is it? There is a world of controversy (well documented) about the doctrinal antagonism between Hegel's notion of the "impersonal" dialectic of world spirit, and Kierkegaard's insistence on the "passionate" primacy of individual belief. The Hegelian dialectic (thesis-antithesis-synthesis) is triadic in form—suitable as a description for directed (teleological) change. Taken into formal religious doctrine, it can be called eschatology. But its priorities are unsuitable for doctrines that want an existential intimacy between individual and deity—such as Kierkegaard demands. My suggestion above—"I believe God \ God believes me"- as it is dyadic, offers intimacy in the actual present, and does not defer it for abstract progress toward an end. This construction is more creative than descriptive, and it goes deeper rather than further—both may be flaws. But it does champion both the individual soul and God in their immediacy—rather than seeing the first as a factor in the development towards the (ultimate realization of) the second—which is consistent with Hegel's "Evolution of Spirit." As a supreme philosopher of history, Hegel takes onto himself the vantage of the "God-eye"—looking down at history from the vantage of process "as-a-cumulative-whole." We find God at the end of time (our time in thought—the world's time in history) when both have discarded the ladder (Wittgenstein's ladder?) of becoming. This is a bit like playing God—although both H and W (through God's grace) may be right. But we do know that, in lesser hands, this doctrine has led to catastrophe. Kierkegaard's main criticism of Hegel is that such a doctrine alienates any intimacy between the individual and God. From our present perspective, we can say that this doctrine alienates reciprocation between state and citizens. The god of "progressive evolution" has no interest in the individual except as a historical functionary. Value is always in the future. The agony of crucifixion—God-as-human—is here denied a role in individual belief and, so, in the mediate reconciliation between the individual and God.

But Kierkegaard was also a sophisticated nineteenth century European. He accepts (for its part) the validity of empirical knowledge. Yet, he is not willing to place "knowing God" into the evidence-based, falsifiable, and necessarily incomplete, procedures of scientific method. He wants the knowing (as my earlier definition suggests) to be real—not only actual. Further—and importantly—he disdains the ceremonial and dogmatic pseudo-epistemology, and the political ambitions, of established churches. Kierkegaard does not believe—as opposed to the absolutism of dogmatic belief—that irresolution (as in questioning life beyond death) that may persist even at the end of "an attempt to know"—shows weakness. For him, rather, it reveals the farthest stretching of (human) truth making—and so, reveals a first harbinger of the eternity that is outside of human experience. But accepting this requires (at least) a two-tiered epistemology: Failure in achieving a unified belief system entails a confession of theoretical inadequacy—or alternatively, the acceptance of separate epistemic structures for each concern at issue—as with science and religion.

Kierkegaard was not much interested in the truth-generating procedures of physics, certainly not in imposing them on matters of spiritual belief—he did not believe that spiritual truths are proven through the logics of physical truth. For the spiritual realm, proof is not needed, but affirmation is—and especially—intensity: What else is there, he asks—when the mortal coil unravels—but to feel, as fully as one can, the having lived of one's life into its death? Kierkegaard offers us a key word for his thesis: "Passion"—which is—or is a sign of—the truth of—the joined existence of life and death. "I believe God \ God believes me." God matters for me, and I do for God—although there may be no one there in the interchange—except for me.

For Kierkegaard, the first consideration is not the "given"—but rather, a "taking." Primacy of belief in God is an act of passion—an epistemic first aggression of belief from which the lesser beliefs necessary for existence are derived. One might present this consequence more narrowly—and say: "from which the beliefs logically sufficient to a particular form of existence are used to support its actual existence." But I leave this open.

Unlike the romantic urgency of Kierkegaard's doctrines, the movement from group worship to individual belief may also show a socially elitist face—where the decorum, sensibilities, and achievements of a person take on the trappings of organized religious belief. Paradoxically, these trappings can identify a like-mannered group who present themselves as exemplifying a finely honed form of belief, suitable to an exclusivist church—open only to those of like status and persuasion.

In a posthumously published critical essay—"The Return of Foxy Grandpa" (NY Rev. of Books, Oct. 8, 2015), T.S. Eliot takes aim at (among others) Alfred North Whitehead's books "Science and the Modern World," and "Religion in the Making." Eliot criticizes Whitehead's attempt to find common ground between "Science" and "Religion" by insisting that there are no such generic understandings—only specific sciences and particular religions whose interests are in the occasional interactions and more usual conflicts with each other. The notion that there is a comprehensive category to which they all putatively belong, is avoided. Eliot sees Whitehead's God as a "Sunday school superintendent in disguise." But God candidates from other thinkers fare no better: Matthew Arnold's is "a power, not ourselves, which makes for righteousness;" William James's is "a power, one of ourselves . . . working with us for our own ends, though neither He nor we know quite what those ends are."

But what Eliot himself offers is not clear. He speaks approvingly of T.E. Hulme's priority, for the religious attitude, of "dogma"—i.e., belief that is accepted unreservedly (however parochially) as truth. But Hulme's all-encompassing dogma is none other than "Original Sin"—"that man is in no sense perfect, but a wretched creature, who can yet comprehend perfection." (So what else is new?) Eliot then mentions Babbitt's doctrine of "grace" as "singularly near to Christianity." (Not to anything else?) Both these—dogma and grace—are then offered as sufficient to bypass the search for the nature of God in the mind of the solitary believer. The "wretchedness of life" may be an empirical finding, and the dogma of "original sin" can serve as an ethical reason (and political excuse) for the existence of "wretchedness." "Grace," however, is different—it is a characteristic of manners—an ability to remain calm and, yes, flexible (dancer-like) in the light of perceived or endured suffering. It is also the manner of the well-born—looking sadly down on starvation in the village—while understanding that it really is the villagers' own doing—they having been given a glimpse of perfection—which they did not act upon.

But in this we find a suggestion—in and for our time—of a coupling: Kierkegaard's "passion" and Eliot's "grace." Neither—on face—have much to do with each other: In the former, God is immediate; in the latter—perhaps irrelevant. Passion, furthermore, can be unmannerly—while grace can go beyond evidence of good breeding into foppery. I do think that Kierkegaard would love to meet God face to face and offer—with both passion and grace—to the sympathetic Host of Heaven—the agonies of his and others' lives. Eliot, however, would be suspicious—waiting for the proper demeanor that God must show to be taken seriously—and only then be invited to the party.

Uneasiness with generic categories, when replaced by dis-related multiple categories, occurs in many present-day venues: "Science" is replaced by "sciences;" "art" by "arts;" a single "morals" by "multiple moralities," the "authority of absolutes" by the "utility of relativisms"—etc. The key theoretical danger here is that these proliferations—moving from singular to plural reference—take the original subject as simply honorary—the categorical requirements of its parts becoming more and more independent of each other. In one such narrative, when "God" is replaced by "Gods"—the move may not be a search for a deeper, more pluralistic understanding of a difficult mystery—but rather, a sign that the pluralities, in their separateness (and self-sufficiency) are closer to the experiences of life than are the generics from which they derive. That there is no God—only Gods—is historically, if not theologically, accurate. The same holds true for the tension between "There is a God" and "There is no God"—positions that have both gathered plaudits, but have also fomented much bloody strife. The ecumenical niceties we occasionally see in meetings of diverse congregations, does not mean that there are serious attempts afoot to merge all religions into one—on the supposition that, if there is a God at all, there is but one God, although one with many names. Don't count on it. The Roman church and the English church try occasionally—but to no avail. The Religions descended from Buddha and Mohammed are coming to have closer affinity to places and politics than to theology: It has become too easy to say: God is what the people (or their representatives) say God is—as long as they vote the right way. The signs suggest that free-market competition reigns between beliefs. If you dislike being burnt at the stake, or you need an abortion—go to another state.

I know a person—a handyman who comes to fix my plumbing or my wiring or my leaky roof. He is a troubled man who finds it hard to cope with a larger world he mostly cannot fix. On occasion we talk, and he tells me of his relationship with Jesus: "Jesus is my best friend—he talks with me and walks with me—and I always feel better—he's always there for me." The man belongs to no church—this being irrelevant to his faith. He does not ask if I know Jesus—for Jesus is his Jesus, not mine. He grows uncomfortable when I ask about his knowledge of God—the term "God" constituting interference—perhaps alluding to the boss of the world he cannot fix—a spoiler to his relationship with his friend Jesus.

Rembrandt made two paintings on the death of Christ: "The Erection Of The Cross," and "The Descent From The Cross" (1632). In both, he includes a background figure with his own features. The "witness" aspect is clear, but in these Baroque spectacles, the roles represented by the players can remain unclear. Is Rembrandt's presence simply devotional—an affirmation of his faith? Or is he playing a role—perhaps acting as God watching the evolution of his own creation? Or is he a disinterested observer from another time and place—watching the small spectacle of a passing act of political passion and doctrinaire sadism. Perhaps Jesus plays multiple roles here as well: As the cross is being lifted up, the figure on it is taunt and symmetrical—a young male body who is also God the Son, fully knowing the before and after of this moment's agony. In the descent, the body is different—curvilinear, almost female—a passivity which I read as the transition to spirit: The lesson of the human phase is complete—preparations for the Last Judgment must begin—praise and blame now, are fully formed. But if one wants a greater evocation of the ferocity and implacability of Judgment—a celestially angry response to the crucifixion—it would be better to turn to the paintings of Michelangelo and Van Eyck.

But I must now confront the question more directly. I have so far been apportioning it to my readings, musings, and the uncertainties of memory: The question is: What is God? A beat-up artist friend of mine—when asked: "What is art?" answered, with a Brooklyn- based patina: "Art is a woid." The answer was brave—but wrong. To say, then, that "God is a word"—would also be wrong. These fin-du-siecle answers—whether despairing, self-serving or just fashionable—are only puddle-deep. The questions won't go away.

I was brought up in the Catholic faith, and found cause, at the age of seventeen, to pronounce myself an atheist. I had friends—at least as crooked as I, who were dong the same. To be an atheist, in those times, was to be free. The reasons were various—but they mostly stemmed from the post-depression squalor, and the depressing religious rituals to which, variously, we as children were condemned to. The question of God was simply one of an increasingly irritating obedience to an irrelevancy. The opportunities of a secular college, and the exposure to other, finer, minds—was (for me) the gate to freedom. The operative question was: Why believe? Why worship what we are not part of? If God is extraneous to us—or we to God—then God does not exist. That lasted a good while. But looking back—"being an atheist," is not- in these latter days—liberating. Indeed, it is reminiscent of free love in tall grasses, making art without looking at past art, joining a collective that is programed to ease your anticipated fall. "God" is not needed in any of these scenarios. But it so happens that world existed before you were born—and will go on after you are dead. Unless you like to flirt with solipsism, you didn't make the world. It might just be that God does. It's worth thinking about.

The real conflict, to my mind, is between self-consciousness and death—not merely consciousness (which "lesser" animals have) and not merely the death that marks the end of an organism's physical life. We know, upon reflection, that we as a species, have historically and uniquely striven for conceptual and material enlargement beyond ourselves—but that as individuals we each must, in our own short order, die. We also know that we, when dead, will not know that we are dead—(although this has been contested). But if acknowledged, it gives some grounds for inveighing against—and rejecting—such referential terms as "Almighty God"—which cast the Deity as superior in self-sufficiency, power, and eternality, to everything we are. We might then slip-slide and ask: "Why him and not me?" Imagine! An imperious God confronted by his jealous creation. (Is this what Lucifer has in mind?) But such a construal, however strained, points to ideals we have developed, and powers we need to convince ourselves, before we die, that we indeed must die. We also must affirm that our living is worth its having. We then have good reason to meditate upon transcendence over dying—upon our actuality become a reality that includes both life and death. This is called—often facetiously—"The meaning of life." But yes! I do propose (if for no other reasons than my personal itch) that asking about the meaning of our living is a good question. But there are other reasons for asking.

The faces (manifestations) of God—throughout the ages—have been simulacra—images, masses, and other theatrical shows—of cultural awareness of God. The (intrinsic) worth—and (perceived) beauty of these images—have attested to the value of the efforts that brought them into being. But, there also (and increasingly) is an indifference to their message (although not their form) that signals the agnostic attitude of practical avoidance: "My, how full each day is—what with everything I have to do—and (as you say) there is a time that is my time of dying. But why bring that up at all? Tacky! Dying is quick and far away—and I've got good genes. So don't bother me now—the meaning of life (whatever that is) can be put off till someone important asks." Evidently, it would be both unsociable and unrewarding, to argue against all that. What could prove such attitudes wrong?—Certainly not popular reason or coercive statutes. Perhaps a change in imagery and ritual might help—but where are the God-infected artists that also make good art?

The serious approach, to my mind, would be a rethinking of the references we make to God—especially, by asking hard questions about the relationship between Divinity and the travails of his (purported) creation. Think of it: The century just past has seen the two most destructive and unforgiving wars in all of history. And against those frightful images, we levy the same tired doctrines of divine right—supported by political power, enlightened self-interest—and so on—that have carried us along since we lived in caves. The more recent additions of historical inevitability, racial or ethnic superiority, and lawful greed, have only added to the misery and provoked more slaughter.

XXXIII

FOUR CONCEPTS OF GOD

AT THIS LATE POINT, I offer four concepts of God—which I believe contain major issues for the belief in Divine Existence:

1) An Interessionist God.

This is a God who reaches (down) to shepherd us through the life created for us, and who gives comfort to our misery, and intercedes through the teachings of clergy, through miracles and other such signs—all in our behalf. Intercession, in this context, is a necessary counter to the imperfections of human will. This is a paternalistic, if benign, construal of the relationship. God is the all-powerful, all knowing, all caring father who instructs the (believing) child in the protocols of living. But this relationship diminishes as the child becomes adult. Free-will is then asserted—ingratitude and disbelief as well. So the intercessionist God (in order to remain God) must document (assert) his own authority—the potency of "divine good" in worldly affairs. Leibnitz gave support for this requirement in his thesis that the world we have is "the best of possible worlds." But however subtle is Leibnitz's logic of parsing "possible," this doctrine has not sat well: Intercession (for the good) is welcome, but life remains unfair. Misery continues unchecked. Is then, God unjust, indifferent, or merely incompetent? The contrast between Hegel's "slaughter bench of history" and God's "benevolence" is too great a chasm to bridge with "intercession." Then too, the paternalistic quality of this form of relationship is disturbing. Must we humans always remain indentured servants—or dependent children? Are we never granted freedom or allowed to grow up? The old models of authority—those upon which such locutions as "God the Father," "God the

King," "Lord," "Master," "Ruler." are based—now grate. The "I—Thou" relationship—the intimacy of love, and the secrets of mutual forgiveness- all this is absent (or, at least not evident) with an intercessionist God.

2) An Interventionist God.

I change the quality (not direction) of the relationship between God and humanity by calling it one of "intervention"- which smacks of unrevealed purposes and motives beyond human understanding. It does work, however, to question the credibility of "omni-benevolence"—of a paternalistic God. In this interpretation, God is a creator whose being is identical with creating, but whose creation—our world—is but a participation in an expanding God-Cosmos, of which it—we and our world—may be but a small part. "Intervention" here, is not a civic or a family affair—as it is with intercession. Here, God's relation to the world is a matter of continuing Divine Purpose by regimenting earthly purposes toward that end. God's purpose is dynamic (which can be variously understood as "cumulative" or, simply, as "continuing"—this second depriving "purpose" of the incentive of a goal. The "free will" attributed to humans is only apparent in both these scenarios—inasmuch as the development of the Cosmos is, within the total span, inexorable. This is not the classic "master-servant" version of the divine-human relationship—in that there are no expectations, no punishment, and no reward—just participation.

In the cumulative (teleological) version of this concept of God, the scenario is modeled after the journey in Hegel's "Phenomenology of Spirit" which, while not proposing (but not denying) a Deity as instigator of the process, nevertheless imparts a historical inevitability to the successive stages. This inevitability is evidenced through the progressive stages of "dematerialization"—and so—"idealization"—of historical change: Pure thought (Geist)—variably translated as mind or spirit, is the end-point. The case—before the beginning and after the ending—is not a concern for Hegel—as Geist extends beyond phenomenal time. One problem with a teleological notion of history—as progress toward some (predetermined) end—is that it describes historical process unevenly. Evidently—knowledge of the physical world increases through time, and each successive accretion is matched by technological invention. Just as evidently—war, suffering, deprivation, continue unabated, each manifestation finding the means necessary for its purposes. We may well ask: If intervention is authoritarian—is it for God's sake or ours? Does God need a "sake?" Why does "our sake" need "God's sake?"

The spiritual ideal of "ascent," while it may fulfill a theoretical need for "completeness" as fulfilled in historical time, does not show that in historical time, normative (moral) progress follows with it. Indeed—from our present vantage—it seems to show the opposite: The greater the population increase, the higher the body-count. To rationalize this imbalance, need we return to the Intercessional God—whose largess is based on criteria of our deserving—or might we just discard the notion of an intrusive god entirely?

3) A Pantheist God.

There is a connection between this theory of inscrutable purpose, and Pantheism. The connection is not apparent—even counter-intuitive, but I believe it to be a way of avoiding the "existence of evil" dilemma that "Intercessionism" leaves us in. To elaborate on this, I use Spinoza's Pantheist theory as a reference. (Tractatus Theologico-Politicus—1670). Spinoza's God is not outside—neither above nor below—the world. Rather, God is (in) the world- more specifically—the natural world. The totality of being—as we can grasp it—is God. The totality of nature—of which we are a part—is God. Dichotomies—as in divine and human, physical and spiritual, (even) good and evil—are rejected. But Spinoza's nature is not a "peaceable kingdom"—it can be brutal and bloody, but also exhilarating in its portents of "wholeness." Spinoza's ethical writings present this notion of wholeness in a way that I call "pan-creativity." Awkward, yes—but it suggests a way of spreading the issues of good and evil, and God's purposes, over the entire map of creation. Spinoza's "evil" is essentially deprivation and passivity—an "inability-unwillingness" to enrich—through the elaboration of present capacity—the potential within a given aspect of being. Rocks and lichens share this with salamanders, dogs and humans. This is an early imprint of the theory of evolution—not to develop is not to cope and, hence, is to disappear. "Consciousness" plays its role in given species—but the theory expands beyond this capacity by embracing all the forms of nature. Praise and blame, good and bad, are not central for this doctrine. They are limited by the larger conflict between privation and creation. Some part of this involves the human will (and hence, praise and blame)—other parts do not. They are subject to what we euphemistically call "natural process." But all of it exemplifies the God that—with all else (us included)—is indeed all of it.

FOUR CONCEPTS OF GOD

The realization for the human mind, that it is part of God, brings the question of Divine Existence into the intimacies of self-question: Why do I—Why do I need to—Do I want to? What does it add to my life to—believe in God? For each of these, there is the impetus to create the God that satisfies. The Pantheist God is the most immediate—yet, the most vulnerable. A God that is synonymous with self as well as with all creation (as best one knows it) is always around. But such a God requires a special kind of attention—one must focus on the eternal that is manifest within the immediate.

All the time? Yes! To illustrate: I have spent time meditating in the company of a large rock nestled in a small stream that flows through moist glades where birds build nests and propagate. Deer come by at intervals and regard me as a friend, as do the mosquitos that (who?) seem to drink less blood than they used to. I have sat there for days that mellow into nights—which have welcomed my presence by showing their unending array of stars. The moon has convinced me that Luna has a face like that of the girl I used to know. But the raccoons (are they not God's creatures too?) opened my cookie jars, and ate all the stew in the black pot that has provided me with the sustenance needed to be whole. The food's now gone; I've run out of money; winter's coming; and I'm getting cold and old. But there's no God to call for help—for God just is what's happening to me. Maybe I'd better go home.

4) An absent God.

The external pervasiveness and internal immediacy of a Pantheistic God does not sit well with the individual for whom, epistemically, the world is a creation of individual consciousness—"the world I know." Or—if taken to a metaphysical extreme, the world (I create) exists as an issue of a solipsistic act—and only as expressions of that act. An absent God is much like that.

God, imaged in this way, may (perhaps—if one can swallow the story) be responsible for creation—but such a God does not (want to) appear in or interfere with, the world's workings. This image is partially compatible with the Hegelian thesis noted above—in that the final stage of the Hegelian development goes beyond orthodox religion into "philosophy." This final stage is to be understood as religion without the sensual trappings (rituals, ornamentations, pious practices) that previously have seemed necessary for the securing of belief. To accept worldly progress without the requirement of an instigating or directing God—is a belief that can be understood as rational—but which contains an underlying practicality that does not (although it can) require the underpinnings of a God. This thesis amounts to a belief in a cosmically implicit process that encompasses creation, development, and consequence—but does not require the necessary existence of a creating deity. But the nature of such a process, in turn, needs further explaining: An absent God may mean no God at all—just an a-theism which takes matters on its own, adds to what needs filling—without either the necessity or the beauty of a belief that living is a consequence of divine will.

There is, in this a-theism, another way of looking at an absent God—this is by putting the onus of the separation on us instead of on God. Here, we can blame the absence of deity on the limits of language—and reinforce these limits by dividing our language into parts: into what can be said, what can sensibly be said, and what cannot (should-not) be said at all. This is Wittgenstein's gambit. It is in the second of these—the sensible part—that we find the values of truth, validity, confirmation—all those required for our efforts to progressively know the physical world. The absence (from this language) of "God" does not seem, practically, to hinder these efforts. But the avoidance does generate a silence about what else is important for our life—about all that we cannot cope with by applying values of truth and falsity. There is a window here: According to the analytic theories we have been discussing, there is much we think about of which we should not speak. But this cannot mean restrictions on what we can (or do) think about. Even the most disciplined mind has errant thoughts. The case has not been made (at least not to my satisfaction) as to why much of what we "can and do" think about—we "cannot" or "should not" speak about.

What would cleansing the language of what Wittgenstein calls nonsense, accomplish—except to put us into a totalitarian zone of linguistic repression—or a society that depends on a formal language, but has no common language—or a society that has no language that is adequate to its life-needs? This last entails the creation of multiple languages—each tailored to fit a shifting need. The "Tower of Babel" reappears. While knowledge of the physical world undoubtedly expands through time, there is the countervailing current—that what we do not want to think about (and will not speak about) is a subtraction from the means (linguistic, emotive, persuasive) with which we have previously coped with the world. There is a gain here—but also a loss here of richness: of focus on and enjoyment of, the intricacies of aberrant descriptions. This shows an academic-puritanical unwillingness to rejoice in the beauty of an image that shows an unwanted conceptual quirk. Bach's Saint Matthew Passion, and the Michelangelo's Sistine Ceiling can then be viewed as faults in understanding. Who could actually believe what is being sung and shown? But then where does that leave us? Poverini immersed in Pap! Yet, there is no doubt that we, in our living, will continue to emulate—through our own images—the discourses of our time. It also seems clear that we gravitate to that discourse that seems to best address our needs—and then, aggressors that we are—we find good reasons to vilify other forms of discourse. But do we—I ask you—have to be satisfied with the images we now make?

The greatest period in Western visual art—from, say, Giotto through Rembrandt—offers incredibly acute sensibilities and astonishing techniques. Yet, all these were largely at the service of extant pomp and power in ways that—were it not for the aesthetic intrusions of grace and beauty—no one now or then (well, almost no one) could appreciate. Modern art—to use a broad brush—replaced the public subject with its self-referential counterpart—art as art—and so released the artist from addressing the beliefs and imperatives of his fragmenting society. This change is evidence, as well, of a theoretical division—between world affairs as they actually proceed, and as God "would want them" to proceed. Equally, it illustrates our present avoidance of the recurring dilemmas of belief: The notion, "God," has suffered so many reductions in confrontations with scientific knowledge, philosophical analysis, and brute fact—not to say the periodically renewed horror of "religious wars"—that what can be said as justification for belief in God—shows a discomfort level that must be met with ambivalence. What was once a fervent dialogue—supported by ritual and exhortation (and much violence, true) has become an academic specialty—"comparative religion." Belief is now a passing thought—directed more at social acceptance that to personal search.

XXXIV

INTERLUDE

I pause here, in the middle of these considerations, to list some ruminations that do not (yet) point to an argument, but which seem, like the insistent fly on a rainy summer's afternoon, to persist in being considered for inclusion—and (my) attention—especially when night begins to fall. I do not respond to them in order, but expect (know) that they and the issues they raise will (do) appear in these pages. (This is a bit of flim-flam on my part. You see—I've already written this book to its end). The effort here is to show that I still respect, and occasionally employ—and exhibit—the power of linear thinking.

These ruminations are:

- Why do we need the notions of closure and completeness for our conception of the universe?
- We can surmise that completeness evidences both harmony and goodness as essential characteristics of creation—and that closure is a process designed (by God) to achieve this. But why do the disorderly many, in a chaotic world, also believe this?

The belief that this is so, is historically recurrent—but this historical characteristic does not address the (basic) question as to whether it is true. Whether there is or is not a God or an afterlife—seems an after-thought.

Not true. This belief is as strong as is the need for knowledge. Well said, Lucian—it sounds like the lyrics for a hymn. But you should know that the composition of hymns more closely mirrors the levels of androgen and estrogen imbalance in given populations than they do the nature of divinity.

INTERLUDE

But if there is no afterlife—and we can prove that (how do we go about doing that?)—then what is the incentive for such belief? Well, we can't really speak about the afterlife while living—especially when we haven't yet been able to describe it. But what better subject is there to occupy you when (as Porgy sings) "You're tired of living but feared of dying."

The incentive for the privileged sector is more indirect: The belief in God, etc., comes out of the social need (perhaps altruistic hope) that love (and its good works) is the (progressively revealed) essential human characteristic.

But if the belief is shaky—if it is just a (deluded) hope—why then should it be believed? Some believe that believing in a benevolent God encourages the political belief that (even in an as yet unjust society) the natural order will trickle divine goodness down to stimulate, and irrigate, earthly plenty.

Must "belief" and "truth" come together in a single judgment in order to be epistemically acceptable? We can never know for sure (except in formal systems for which we ourselves provide the rules) whether our beliefs are true—or, as in other cases, merely warranted. "Truth" is a function of linguistic systems. To require "truth" of statements about the physical world is to accept contingent truths as sufficient for belief—even though these can always be falsified. Truths about God, immortality, ultimate meaning—all require a different notion of truth—one that is beyond formal language, but not beyond our experience as contingent beings. Metaphysical truth is not empirical truth—it is more pervasive, sometimes more persuasive, but historically less efficient. To my mind, it is best to leave these truths (and their internal variants) separate within the contexts where they flourish. But this should not discourage dialogue or dinner-parties. Such dialogue should be directed to no preconceived end—as befits the nature of conception and creation.

Can the many realms that require truth-judgments for their plausibility, e.g., Logic, science, philosophy, religion, ethics, politics, art, all have different forms and determinations of truth as a basis for judgment. If so apportioned, "truth" is in danger of joining the panoply of suspect judgments that empower the workings of various social categories and their members. Here I offer a preliminary list of suspects: "Taste," "Virtue," "Country," "Freedom," "Work," "Family," "Success." Such desiderata all require a conjunction of "true" and "good"—even though the grounds for this conjunction have not, in every case, been specified. In common parlance, it's fairly easy to do: One can say: "It's true that doing X is good"—and then (if X is a generally accepted virtue) we can leave it there. But if we substitute—for X: "It is true that God is good," then we should—even in common parlance—also supply the evidence that this is so. Pointing to the wealth of empires is not adequate as evidence—there are too many occasions countervailing. But if we point to the human soul—in its journey from innocence to wisdom—life and death—then we might find a place for such a statement.

XXXV

LOVE AND DEATH

I ONCE SAW A TV interview with the late Pope John-Paul where he was asked the question—"What is God?" He replied that the answer is very difficult—but one thing we know—"God is love."

Embarrassing—no? Such a reification of a sentiment we are now so uneasy about, that—in boardroom and in bed—it is relegated to tacky magazines, and self-help morning shows. "Love," as it seems, is just about as difficult to define as "God."

Yet, it might prove a good starting point. "No-one knows what love is" say the these-days surface-skimmers. But there were other times and other loves: "The love that passeth all understanding." is an impassioned wave at the ineffable. "Medieval—courtly love" (no touching allowed) is defined through prescribed (and proscribed) gestures and marked by rolling eyes, jousts, and public sweating. Yet the greatest exponents of serious touching—even in the courtly tradition (and immortalized in music and literature) are Tristan and Isolde. "Romantic love" is sentimentally replete with shivering protestations between starving artists and consumptive girlfriends. This was later remedied (as art prices rose) by a secular move from condemnation to tolerance—"if only those misfits are willing to behave—and wash—we'll invite them to our (their) showing."

We—here and now—often confuse love with sex. What else (we say) but sex do we have—when we contrast it with the dreary self-esteem offered us by psychotherapy, or the impassioned letters of barely-remembered conquests that we keep hidden in our study? Love does seem far away when we watch the indifferent eyes of our partner in that sexy resort in Malibu—there we can avoid the confusion. But lest you think that, in my old age, I've become a geriatric blue-nose, let me right-now say that

I'm for both sex and love—whenever and wherever the two come together. The self-righteous path is not good as a way to love. It's also a disaster for sex. Separation of duties in a marriage is not an aphrodisiac, nor is the looser requirement of "quality time" (a meager substitute for both love and sex) when such is undertaken to mollify the strains of chores and profits through weekend outings.

"Love," then, seems to have the same problems as "God." There are too many attributes, too much contradiction, evasion, and delusion. But there also (as with God) is a lot of history. These difficulties can have both issues degenerate into the quasi-solution of category-denial: "God doesn't exist, therefore, there is no such thing as Love." In actuality, we only have characteristic attitudes that, given one's concerns, can be called "loving" or "believing." But both terms, if one does not have these concerns (Zombie-chic)—can be abandoned altogether. What a relief—as the tabloids say—to never again have to say: "I love you." The expression "God is Love," then, can be taken as an assault on present-day sensibilities, by insisting on the alliance between two now fragile (almost obsolete) entities—one called loving, the other God. But 'love' can also be taken as a referentially suspect, hence dangerous, term. The extant wisdom is to act upon our suspicions and deny the reality of both components and, hence, the cogency of the pairing. This will keep us protected from the perils of an earlier time.

But before I go—and while we are both still here—I want to raise some further issues about other (suspect) pairings.

One pairing I have in mind does not have the common ground indicated above, but does has the advantage of (some) empirical respectability as regards the nature of the contrast. I refer here to the Freudian posit of the interplay between Love and Death—"Eros and Thanatos." (Gesammelte Werke, XIII). The issue taken up is the conflict between the physical drive towards reproduction (pleasure), and the mental apprehension (fear) of its ending. Freud (influenced perhaps by Jung) locates these states in all of nature rather than limiting them to the specific inter-awareness between human existence and consciousness. The evolution of species, fecundity, predation, natural disasters, wars, blooming and withering, lust, disgust, youth and aging—all evidence these opposing functions of creation and death through physical time. In the human context, these oppositions lose their naturalistic transparency. Freud's psychic levels—Id, Ego, Superego—are opaque in their workings: Sexual arousal can turn to domination rather than love—to love expressed as domination—or to domination accepted

LOVE AND DEATH

as love. If these do not satisfy, the self (itself) splits into I and Me—master and slave, hunter and prey, judge and accused. Suicide, in this context, is an act of aggression (retribution) by the Me against the I; murder is aggression (self-defense) by the I against the Other—which often resembles the Me.

I propose to align these terms—love and death—into a dialectic whose synthesis is God. So aligned, the dualism—if destabilized—becomes a triad. This in turn shows the strategy of sublation—where impasse is resolved by a pulling back in order to diagonally advance—but where the goal thus reached is itself undermined when a further stasis threatens, and a new sublation is required. God, in this scheme, is subject to redefinition as the concept becomes inadequate. "God" is a process term. This proposal, of course, is the Hegelian strategy of dialectic—it is also a fair description of human living and believing.

Love is both suspect and indeterminate—as is death—but in different ways. Love shows itself in many of these ways—so many that we wonder (in our vulnerable moments) what, in fact, is being shown and what of this can be possessed. There are many symptoms—some of which (Satan again?) are misleading: The feverishness attributed to love can also be caused by the flu—or its heights and depths mimicked by an incipient bi-polarity. Love's longings can be squandered on a go-go dancer—or a loquacious but aging professor. Such ventures may amount to nothing—which, of course, you didn't know before you started dreaming. But they can be instructive to the praxis evidenced by the fluidity of mating when compared with the stasis of dying. The two are not in balance—movement is required.

The feelings that are causal to the symptoms of love are not stable in themselves. They only become so through their translation into picturing and description. A historical note here: The sight of a woman's bare ankle would send Victorian hopefuls into paroxysms of (usually unrequited) desire. The casual nudity in the brothels sent them quite a different message—which bolstered the larger distinction (then needed) between lust and love.

I confess that I have felt myself many times to be in love—and most times have been fooled. But feeling and fooling are not the same: One wants to give feelings a metaphysical authenticity—but not the fooling. The latter is a happenstance, requiring further education. But the feelings, however often fooled, are a conceptual achievement of which they are a reference. But they cannot, because of their fluidity, reveal an essence. The need for movement toward the truth of the matter of love continues.

ISSUES AND FRAGMENTS

The physical symptoms of love—more so than those of death—are commonplace in this sexually voyeuristic age. And they are procurable for our wonderment—entertainment—delectation—information—self-castigation—debasement—selective emulation—at all levels of public scrutiny. Love, in contrast, does not have an actual face—as it is not a physical condition. Its manifestations, therefore, are given it by the images historically devised to do it honor—for it continues to be, despite its physical prolixity, pervasively important. In this sense, love is a mirror of the faces we have given to the many aspects of God.

I turn now to a consideration of Death—the other component in my definition of God. Death, like love, is indeterminate in that it has two aspects—actual death and real death. Actual death is the body dying—consciousness perishing together with its flesh. This is the disclaimer for materialists—they offer no notion of transubstantiation: The physical and spiritual realms are in no need of integration. Following this vein, I can offer other disclaimers that follow along: There is no resurrection of the body, no bodily ascension, no roasting in eternal fire as punishment—nor is there ascent, guided by the breath of incense, toward an eternal reward. Further—back here—there is no pre-destination that shows in the face of your neighbor—no evasive look that gives you the excuse to turn him in. Even within the best of worlds, there are none upon whom the Divine Light preferentially shines—despite the massive contributions made over the centuries to assure this favor.

To continue my disclaimers: There is no parade after Armageddon of bodies freshly risen—despite their ancient times of moldering—brought into the celestial courtroom for the weighing of their final worth, and their eternal fate—adjudicated through the well-tempered scales of the last judgment. But I ask you: Why should the end of life be a courtroom?

Real (not actual) death has other problems: What is the nature of real—as opposed to actual—death? The salvage attempted here—of a construal of immortality—may be just a fabrication, a mere tuck-pointing of a crumbling theory. But I hope otherwise. I have described real death as ongoing memory of everything one has touched or been touched by—brought into games that are played but never completed. Such games, as I imagine them, do not end—but continue their play in the place I call "New Purgatory." Playing the game provides for immortality—not actual but real—in the sense that one's once-lived life, when played, does not dissolve into nothingness. A caveat is necessary here. "Immortality" requires consciousness and its history. When full consciousness (the world) ends, immortality ends as well—for there is no longer the collectivity of the living and the dead—and no further transformations of the game—to keep it going. There is then no need ("need" requiring consciousness) and no place ("place" requiring perception) for the distinction being made here—between actual and real.

Actually, the life one really lives is beyond one's own consciousness even when one is alive. It consists—not only of those aspects of your living you don't yourself remember, but of everything that would or would not be, had you not lived at all. Real death is not only the completeness of having actually lived, but of everything that has occurred because you lived. The life that is actually lived—this life does not die but, having relinquished consciousness, becomes real—for it is continually reconstructed as it diffuses into history and is joined with other histories. As this process is never complete—as long as there are others—it can be called immortal.

I believe that "God" does not extend beyond my dying—although God may. (This again is a distinction between 'actual' and 'real'). The God I know—the actual one—began as a taste of otherness outside me when I was born, continued on as a provider, teacher, confidant and scold as I grew older—and now ends as a testy disputant who has also had a share of worse and better days. In truth—we, God and I—are both disappointed in each other. We now—as existences—must part: I to die, and God to where the thinking I once did, and never fully spoke when living, cannot follow. This seems right: God does not die. So, to talk about the death of God when one is alive is absurd: What would you do, friend Nietzsche, without the continuing liveliness of the subject you once thought you talked to death. But to expect God to follow you into your death is absurd: God is not there—no more, actually, than are you.

While alive—I hold that God is a synthesis of love and death—of the expansiveness of loving and the closure of dying. Experiencing God requires a synthesis of the actual and the real—of the physical world and the theoretical world of dreams and memory. Although there should be no confusion between these pairs in the Divine Mind (God being the ultimate source and arbiter of "should") there remains—in the living mind—the urge (a game God does not play) to explain the one by the other. "Explaining" is a game of the living—explanation has only partial reference to a subject within any instance of a life. But the act itself is optimistic. Each game generates a later game designed to explain the earlier game. Finding linkages between explanations is itself a game—it is called history.

Memory, like explanation (and history) is also partial. As the world cannot be completely explained, so the past cannot be completely retrieved. But as one's past and the world's past are intertwined, we remain alive through playing the games of memory and recollection. The totality of the world's past, however, is larger than the sum of collective memories—for, however hard we look, for however long—there are contents of the past outside the ones we know. The totality of the past is a metaphysical realm beyond history.

The future is also a metaphysical realm, for it is the totality of all things possible. To use an analytic term: We can "project" possible scenarios of the future with varying degrees of success. But the future—as totality—is neither actual nor possible—not only because it isn't here yet—but because the world(s) of the future are not the same as the ones we project—just as the world of our past is not the same as the one we recollect. The "totality" of the future is a misnomer—for the "possible worlds" that constitute it are not finite in number. We always add (despite our need for actuals) to the collection of possibles that might be. This is a more extreme epistemic disclaimer than saying some possibles will become actual and some will not. The game of prediction is not a lottery—no-one here and now can win.

Having made this attempt to dematerialize both past and future, let me now amend my statement above—that "God requires a synthesis of the "Actual" and the "Real." The actual (empirical) world that marks our lives is a part of the real world (of memories and dreams)—and in this sense, we can say—like Spinoza—that "we are part of God." This is true—as far as it goes. But I now say that knowing God requires the synthesis between the realms of "Past" and "Future"—taken as metaphysical totalities—together with the lesser synthesis, we existentially attempt to make, between the realms I call the "Actual" and the "Real."

Earlier, I defined my proffered realm—the "New Purgatory"—as a joining of life-events: Our memories, and the memories that others have of us. This is the realm of the "Real"—but it discloses an ongoing (trans-historical) instability: Memories expand and contract—are added to, revised, and lost. Yet, this instability—the transformations within reality—is also the continuation of (real) life after our (actual) death. In this sense, we can say: "We continue after death." The New Purgatory is both realm and game—it contains the variables of our real lives, and plays the games of their interactions. No—it is not all there is—there is always something new for the burning. (Even when dead, we are "becoming.") But when subsumed within (neither over nor under) the metaphysical totalities of past and future, Purgatory is the realm of Creation and Creator—what and where God is. Given this "eternity in motion," we do not need the dangling antinomies of Heaven and Hell.

XXXVI

A LAST FRAGMENT

At that distant point in the physical evolution of the world—where all consciousness ends—when expansion has turned irrevocably to reduction—with all things living and once alive having gone to embers—and there is no more "going" left—the question can (now—not then) be asked about that eventuality: whether at that point there (still) is a God.

I cannot answer the question—and I don't think anyone can—because about it, come that time—there will be no one and no time. Neither will there be the call of memory, the need for explanation, nor the anticipation of another game: We will all be silent.

As the lovers sang when parting: Addio—senza rancor.

www.ingramcontent.com/pod-product-compliance
Lightning Source LLC
Chambersburg PA
CBHW050806160426
43192CB00010B/1656